D0212818

The Institute of Accounts

This book focuses upon the Institute of Accounts (IA), an organization to which the modern United States' accounting profession can trace its roots. The IA was organized in the early 1880s in New York City and, as discussed in this book, attracted a diverse membership that included some of the leading accounting thinkers of the period. *The Institute of Accounts* describes the association's early development, its usefulness to the needs of bookkeepers and accountants in the late nineteenth century, and its historical importance.

The book begins with an introduction, which is followed by a description of the organization, its goals, its membership classifications, and its professional characteristics. The authors then discuss the problems facing bookkeepers and accountants in the late nineteenth century and the usefulness of the IA in addressing the needs of its members. This is followed by consideration of how the thinking of IA leaders about the nature of accounting knowledge for many years unified the IA's membership by providing answers not only to questions of theory and practice, but also to how this knowledge could play a role in assisting government and business leaders more effectively to order a society experiencing substantial flux. The authors go on to analyze the factors leading to the IA's decline after the enactment of the first CPA law. The book concludes with a consideration of the legacy of the IA.

The Institute of Accounts will be essential reading for accounting historians.

Stephen E. Loeb is the Ernst & Young Alumni Professor of Accounting and Business Ethics at the Robert H. Smith School of Business, University of Maryland. He was formerly co-editor of the *Journal of Accounting and Public Policy* and is the Historian of the Maryland Association of Certified Public Accountants, Inc. **Paul J. Miranti, Jr.** was formerly the Associate Dean for Faculty and Research at Rutgers Business School. He is the author of *Accountancy Comes of Age: The Rise of an American Profession, 1886–1940* (1990), and co-author of *A History of Corporate Finance* (1997).

Routledge New Works in Accounting History
Series editors
*Richard Brief, Leonard N. Stern, School of Business, New York
University, Garry Carnegie, Deaking University, Australia
John Richard Edwards, Cardiff Business School, UK
Richard Macve, London School of Economics, UK*

*This title also features in "The Monograph Series of the Academy of
Accounting Historians," selected by The Academy of Accounting
Historians.

The Monograph Series of the Academy of Accounting Historians
Edited by
O. Finley Graves

The Institute of Accounts

Nineteenth-century origins of
accounting professionalism in the
United States

Stephen E. Loeb and
Paul J. Miranti, Jr.

Routledge
Taylor & Francis Group

LONDON AND NEW YORK

First published 2004
by Routledge
11 New Fetter Lane, London EC4P 4EE

Simultaneously published in the USA and Canada
by Routledge
29 West 35th Street, New York, NY 10001

Routledge is an imprint of the Taylor & Francis Group

© 2004 Stephen E. Loeb and Paul J. Miranti, Jr.

Typeset in Sabon by Wearset Ltd, Boldon, Tyne and Wear
Printed and bound in Great Britain by TJ International Ltd, Padstow,
Cornwall

British Library Cataloguing in Publication Data
A catalogue record for this book is available from the British Library

Library of Congress Cataloging in Publication Data
Loeb, Stephen E.
    The Institute of Accounts : nineteenth-century origins of accounting
professionalism in the United States / Stephen E. Loeb and Paul J.
Miranti, Jr.
        p. cm.
    1. Institute of Accounts. 2. Accountants – United States. 3.
Accountants – Professional ethics – United States. I. Miranti, Paul J.
II. Title.

    HF5616. U5L64 2004
    657' .06'073–dc21   2003013316

ISBN 0-415-28874-6

To Cynthia Loeb, who makes everything possible
and
to Adrienne Gnassi, with love

Contents

Foreword

In *The Institute of Accounts: Nineteenth-Century Origins of Accounting Professionalism in the United States*, Professors Loeb and Miranti provide an intriguing interpretation of the significance of the Institute of Accounts (IA). The authors have developed their analysis on the basis of a scholarly consideration of existing sources relating to the IA. They point out that the IA established the prototype of the characteristics of the modern professional accounting association. Further, Loeb and Miranti discuss the IA's contribution to the development of accounting knowledge and the use of that knowledge to educate accountants and bookkeepers, especially in the late nineteenth century. Throughout the discussion, they consider the role of key individuals such as Charles Ezra Sprague, Henry Harney, A.C. Kittredge, and Charles Waldo Haskins.

The authors discuss factors that they believe resulted in the IA apparently becoming a non-operating entity by 1920. More specifically, faced with having to adapt to the needs of a young and dynamic public accounting profession, the authors suggest that the IA chose to nationalize its traditional direction and thus ceased to function as a leader of change. Further, Loeb and Miranti point out that in an era when specialist associations were, for a variety of reasons, needed, the IA remained a generalist association. The authors neatly tie together the significance of the merger in the early 1940s of both the IA and the National Society of Certified Public Accountants into the

American Institute of Accountants. Also, the authors raise the question as to whether or not the birth of the AICPA should, given those mergers, really be considered to be 1882, when the IA was founded.

The IA was a key early association and contributed mightily to the early development of the accounting profession in the United States. The Academy of Accounting Historians is pleased to have this book as part of its monograph series and thanks Routledge for its publication.

O. Finley Graves, Editor
The Monograph Series of the Academy of
Accounting Historians

Acknowledgments

A number of individuals assisted in gathering material, including Augustine Duru, Fatma Cebenoyan, and Donal Byard. We are indebted to the staff of the American Institute of Certified Public Accountants library for their assistance. We benefited from the comments of Finley Graves and other individuals who reviewed earlier versions of the manuscript. Also, we are indebted to Wilasinee Kiatapiwat, Jonathan Eckhardt, Augustine Duru, Nerissa Brown, and Donal Byard for their comments on one or more earlier drafts of this manuscript. Our thanks to James McKinney for providing a reference that led us to Wilkinson (1908). We would like to express our gratitude to Finlay Graves and Richard Brief who were instrumental in advancing this study. Our thanks also to Anthony Krzystofik for source ideas. Also, we thank Carl Gillingham, our copy-editor, Sarah Coulson, our production editor, as well as Amritpal Bangard and Yeliz Ali for their advice and efforts in bringing this manuscript to publication. Our thanks also to Isobel McLean for her work on the index.

Steve Loeb is Historian and for a number of years was Chair of the History Committee of the Maryland Association of Certified Public Accountants, Inc. and thanks that association and its staff, which over the years have supported and encouraged his history research, including this manuscript. Steve Loeb is appreciative of the outstanding research milieu of the Accounting and Information Assurance area of the Robert H. Smith

School of Business of the University of Maryland, which is due to Dean Howard Frank and Chair James Bedingfield.

* * *

Paul Miranti wishes to acknowledge the intellectual debt he owes to many scholars whose ideas and insights have helped to sharpen his thinking about the relationship between organizations and the professions in recent American history. Foremost in this regard is Louis Galambos who, in his influential studies dealing with the emergence of the "organizational synthesis" in American historiography, broke new ground by stressing the vital role of the professions and their specialized knowledge in shaping contemporary society. Paul Miranti also wishes to thank the following colleagues for sharing their perspectives about the nature of professional dynamics: Andrew Abbott, William H. Becker, Richard P. Brief, James Don Edwards, Dale Flesher, Peter Gray, Gerry N. Grob, Kenneth L. Lipartito, Keith McMillan, Barbara D. Merino, Louis H. Orzack, Gary J. Previts, George Romeo, Claudia Tyska, and Patricia Watson.

Paul Miranti also wishes to acknowledge those who have made his academic home, Rutgers Business School – Newark and New Brunswick, an excellent locale for historical inquiry. This project was facilitated by the support and encouragement of Presidents Richard L. McCormick and Francis L. Lawrence, Vice President for Academic Affairs Joseph J. Seneca, Executive Vice President Norman Samuels, Provost Steven J. Diner, Deans George Benson and Howard P. Tuckman, and Department Chair Dan Palmon.

* * *

In addition, we thank the following for permission to use material: Deloitte & Touche; Hill and Wang, a division of Farrar, Straus and Giroux, LLC (for Wiebe, 1967); Professor Thomas L. Haskell; Blackwell Publishing, Inc./Southwestern

Social Science Association (for Miranti, 1988); American Institute of Certified Public Accountants, Inc.; Keith P. McMillan; and the *Business History Review*. Pictures in Figures 2.1 and 2.2 courtesy of the Library of Congress.

1 Introduction

Many who have studied the evolution of the professions in the United States (U.S.) have focused on how changes in defining cognitive processes have often induced modification of institutions and organizations which govern these fields (e.g., Kohler, 1982; Kohlstedt, 1976). This impetus for change was apparent during the last quarter of the nineteenth century when new problems brought about by rapid "industrialization, mechanization, [and] urbanization" (Wiebe, 1967, p. 12) created opportunities for many classes of experts to demonstrate the usefulness of their knowledge in ordering society.[1] The prestige of the more successful of these groups grew by formulating new paradigms that proved effective in achieving a smoother integration of a polity whose elements were becoming "more complex and interdependent" (Miranti, 1990, p. 9).[2]

In some cases new ways of thinking radically changed professional hierarchies. This was most dramatically evinced in the social sciences and medicine. In the former case the once preeminent American Social Science Association (ASSA) was replaced by specialty organizations (Haskell, 1977; Galambos, 1983, p. 487; Ross, 1991, p. 63; Lipartito and Miranti, 1996, p. 1408; McMillan, 1998b, pp. 57, 85; 1999, p. 26). Similarly, the more vibrant knowledge base of medical science reduced the influence of practitioners of hydropathy and practitioners of herbal medicine (see the general discussion in Kett, 1968, chapters 4–5; see, e.g., Lipartito and Miranti, 1998, p. 305; Burrow, 1977, chapter 5).

The extension of knowledge also transformed institutional structures by creating opportunities for more specialized practice. The extension of medical knowledge, for example, led to the rise of a host of specialties such as anesthesiology, neurology, psychiatry, surgery, and radiology (see Rosenberg, 1987; Starr, 1982; Stevens, 1971). This trend was also evident in engineering where the traditional civil and mechanical applications broadened to encompass innovative aeronautical, automotive, chemical, electrical, and mining specializations (see the discussion in Calhoun, 1960 especially pp. v–xi; Calvert, 1967; Spence, 1970). The scope of civil law also became further differentiated into, for example, anti-trust, bankruptcy, copyright, maritime, patent, securities, and tax practice (e.g., see the general discussion in Abel, 1989, pp. 122–123, 202–204; Lipartito, 1990).

Although the question of how the expansion of knowledge affected organizational growth and decay has been central to studies of many professions (see, e.g., Haskell, 1977; Kett, 1968), it generally has been overlooked in analyzing the evolution of accounting. Instead, two other lines of inquiry have predominated in considering accounting (see the discussion in Lipartito and Miranti, 1998, pp. 302–303). Broadly consistent with the perspectives of Parsonian sociology (see Parsons, 1960), one school has stressed how knowledge professional roles and functions assist in the development of organizations and market structures (see the discussion in Miranti, 1993b, pp. 117–119; Lipartito and Miranti, 1998, p. 302). Some of these scholars have considered how accounting communicates information that is useful in managerial decision-making or regulatory processes (e.g., Fleischman *et al.*, 1991; Garner, 1954; Johnson and Kaplan, 1987; Levenstein, 1991; Miranti, 1989; Oakes and Miranti, 1996); others have focused on the evolution of accounting knowledge and professional forms and their relationship to the rise of capital markets (e.g., Edwards, 1960; Flesher and Flesher, 1986; Previts and Merino, 1979;

Zeff, 1984); others have analyzed how public accountants have interacted with other groups to secure a safe harbor for their specialized skills (e.g., Lee, 1995; Miranti, 1986b); while still others have studied the growth of practice units and/or how professional organizations developed (e.g., Allen and McDermott, 1993; Carnegie, 1993; Howitt, 1966; Jones, 1981; Shackleton, 1995; Walker, 1988).[3]

In contrast, a second line of inquiry has drawn on postmodernist philosophy scholarship, as reflected in the work of Foucault (1972, 1973a, 1973b, 1979) who stressed the importance of analyzing social, cultural, and economic constructions to discover dimensions that were related to politics (see the discussion in Miranti, 1993b, p. 120; Lipartito and Miranti, 1998, pp. 302–303). In this context the objective of this line of accounting research was to deconstruct these constructions to reveal the ways that they were employed to allocate scarce social resources such as income, status, and wealth (see the discussion in Miranti, 1993b, p. 120). As suggested in Miranti (1993b, p. 120), some accounting scholars guided by this critical perspective have emphasized the role of accounting as a disciplinary force in society (Knights and Collinson, 1987; Loft, 1986; Miller and O'Leary, 1987); some accounting scholars have been concerned with the ways that professional institutions have been employed to secure strength in the marketplace (Richardson, 1989; Willmott, 1986); while still other accounting scholars have sought to demonstrate how accounting knowledge could be used to strengthen particular social structures (e.g., Arrington and Francis, 1989; Lehman, 1992; Tinker, 1984).[4]

In this book we evaluate an important "transitional" (see Galambos, 1983, p. 487) accounting organization, the Institute of Accounts (IA) (see flowchart in Figure 1.1), an organization that recently has attracted scholarly interest (McMillan, 1998b, 1998c, 1999; Kyj and Romeo, 1997; Romeo and Kyj, 1998).[5] The IA was founded in 1882 ("Institute of Accountants and Book-keepers of the City of New York," 1882, p. 248), and like the ASSA, was "a generalist body" (Miranti, 1993a, pp. viii–ix; see the discussion in both Galambos, 1983, p. 487 and McMillan, 1998b, pp. 57, 85; 1999, p. 26).

In our analysis we focus primarily on the IA's record of professionalization as chronicled in several contemporary periodicals. The use of these periodicals and other secondary sources has been driven by two unifying questions. First, what role, from the perspective of the IA, did accounting knowledge play in business and social ordering? And, second, what insight does the IA's experience provide about the professionalization of the U.S. accounting occupation. The IA's brief history of leadership is significant because it came at a time of social and cultural change as the U.S. was becoming a more urban and industrialized nation (see the discussion in Miranti, 1990, pp. 8–9, 25, 32). Our approach does not rely on either line of inquiry noted above. We take a more eclectic approach in our analysis but at times draw on both.

In our analysis we discuss how the IA's programs for enhancing knowledge and providing economic benefits were successful in attracting a membership composed of bookkeepers, business managers, educators, and public accountants. We discuss how these programs, however, eventually proved insufficient to members holding certified public accountant (CPA) certificates who wanted to exploit growing opportunities for providing audit services made possible by a nearly decade-long industrial merger boom starting in the mid-1890s (e.g., see the discussion in Allen and McDermott, 1993, p. 20; Lamoreaux, 1985, chapter 1; Wilkins, 1989, pp. 542–543; Miranti, 1990, p. 49).

Also, we discuss how the IA in the early 1890s became a key player, along with the rival American Association of Public Accountants (AAPA), in the political process that led in 1896 to the establishment of a state-sanctioned certified public accountant designation in the State of New York. We discuss how the success of this campaign, however, proved detrimental to the long-term viability of the IA. Although the IA continued until 1940, when the IA and the American Institute of Accountants (AIA) – today the American Institute of Certified Public Accountants (AICPA) – merged (Webster, 1954, p. 14) (see

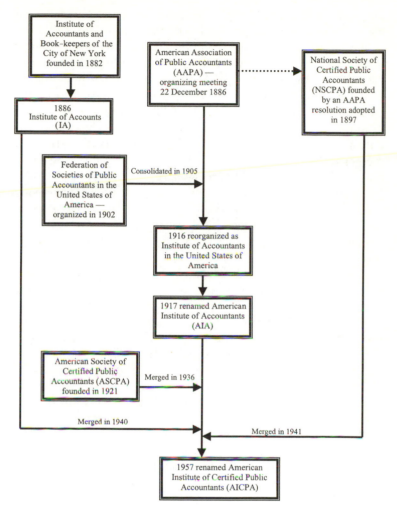

Figure 1.1 The origins of the American Institute of Certified Public Accountants: 1882–1957.

Sources: See citations and discussion in notes 5, 6 and 31 and also at other points in the book.

Figure 1.1 and note 6), the IA declined rapidly as a professional force after the passage of certified public accounting legislation in New York State in 1896. We note that it was this legislative achievement and the IA's subsequent unwillingness to make "the [CPA] movement" (Wilkinson, 1903, pp. 414, 460) a primary associational concern that appears to have created the incentive for a number of the IA's CPA members to shift their primary allegiance to organizations dedicated exclusively to the advancement of their new symbol of professional merit. The merger of the IA with the AIA, however, raises the possibility that the lineage of the AICPA dates to 1882 rather than 1887 (the year the AAPA was incorporated) as has been traditionally assumed (see Loeb, 2002c, p. 19; 2002e, p. 161).[6] The persuasiveness of this latter argument is enhanced when one considers the professional legacy that the IA left for future generations of accountants.

The analysis of the significance of the IA's experience is presented in five steps. In Section 2 we describe the origins of the organization, its goals, its membership classifications, and its professional characteristics. Section 3 discusses problems facing bookkeepers and accountants in the late nineteenth century and the usefulness of the IA in addressing the needs of its members. Next, we explain in Section 4 how the thinking of IA leaders about the nature of accounting knowledge for many years unified the IA's membership by providing answers not only to questions of theory and practice, but also how this knowledge could play a role in assisting government and business leaders in more effectively ordering a society experiencing substantial flux. Section 5 analyzes the factors leading to the IA's decline after the enactment of the first CPA law. Section 6 discusses the legacy of the IA.

2 Origins, goals, membership, and professional characteristics

Associational origins

The IA was "incorporated" 28 July 1882 as the Institute of Accountants and Book-keepers of the City of New York ("Institute of Accountants and Book-keepers of the City of New York.," 1882, p. 248). On 16 July 1886, the Institute of Accounts ("Change of Name.," 1886, p. 30). Although the IA played a leading role in establishing CPA legislation in the 1890s, during its formative years the IA had multiple goals that are mentioned next and discussed in more detail later in our book. On one level the organization was dedicated to education and the advancement of accounting knowledge, while on another level it sought palpable economic benefits for its members (see, e.g., "Institute of Accountants and Book-keepers.," 1882b, pp. 189–190). Such a blending of goals proved effective in attracting a diverse membership, which included, for example, bookkeepers, business managers, and public accountants (see Webster, 1954, pp. 13–14; "Our Portraits," 1883, pp. 65–67).

A call to establish a representative association for bookkeepers and accountants was first registered through articles apparently written by an editor in a specialized journal, *The Book-Keeper.*, edited by Selden R. Hopkins, a public accountant, and also, soon after that journal's founding, by Colonel Charles Ezra Sprague, the secretary and later president of the

Union Dime Savings Bank (see "Book-keepers' Associations.," 1880, p. 166 and "Mutual Association for Book-keepers.," 1881, pp. 17–19; also see, e.g., "The Book-keeper.,"1880a, p. 8; 1880b, p. 56; "Charles E. Sprague, Ph.D.," 1897, p. 129; "Selden R. Hopkins . . .," 1880, p. 159; Webster, 1954, p. 12). Both of these individuals are discussed in more detail later in our book. In describing the goals of the proposed organization, editorials in *The Book-Keeper* indicated that it was not intended to function as a trade union, with the enhancement of member compensation as the only goal ("Book-keepers' Association and Employers.," 1881, pp. 40–41). Instead, the proposed entity was conceived in part as an agency for business people that would provide information about trustworthy and competent bookkeepers and in part as a vehicle that would serve to educate members ("Mutual Association for Book-keepers.," 1881, p. 17). In addition, another benefit thought achievable was the provision of life insurance as had been earlier done by the telegraph operators association for "the Western Union Telegraph Company" ("Book-keepers' Association and Employers.," 1881, p. 41; also see "Mutual Association for Book-keepers.," 1881, p. 17). A later article suggested the establishment of a cooperative credit association for clerks, bookkeepers, and accountants to provide financing for member home purchases (Safely, 1881, pp. 120–121).

These appeals eventually succeeded in attracting 37 founding members, and at a meeting on 8 June 1882 the group selected "Edward C. Cockey, storekeeper, Western Union Telegraph Co.," as its "President" and also selected an "Executive Council," an "Examining Committee" to evaluate the suitability of applicants to the association, and a "Board of Audit" ("Institute of Accountants and Book-keepers.," 1882a, p. 173; also see "Institute of Accountants and Book-keepers.," 1882b, pp. 190–192). An early goal was to attract "at least two per cent. of the 20,000 book-keepers" estimated to be in the environs of New York City ("The First Annual Meeting of the Institute of Accountants and Book-keepers of the City of New York.," 1883, p. 97). It is possible that this degree of market penetration was selected partly because it represented a minimum estimated threshold number necessary to support the aforementioned life insurance program which at that point had not begun ("Mutual Association for Book-keepers.," 1881, p. 17; "The First Annual Meeting of the Institute of Accountants and Book-keepers of the City of New York.,"1883, p. 97). Although precise figures are lacking, one authoritative source estimated a membership in excess of 80 at the apex of the Institute's fortunes (Webster, 1954, p. 13). As is discussed later, Wilkinson (1908, p. 49) indicates that circa 1908 the IA had around 135 members (also see Romeo and Kyj, 1998, p. 44 n. 17). However, as is also discussed later, during the second decade of the twentieth century, the IA probably became dormant.

Association's goals

The "objects and purposes" (goals) of the new organization outlined in both its "Charter-Paper" and its "By-Laws" were varied and likely designed to attract a broad spectrum of individuals ("Institute of Accountants and Book-keepers.," 1882b, pp. 189–190). The overall goal of the IA was "the elevation of the profession, and the intellectual advancement and improvement of its members" ("Institute of Accountants and Book-keepers.," 1882b, p. 189). This overall goal was reflective of the perspective of Colonel Sprague, a man of wide intellectual interests who received an undergraduate degree as well as a masters and an honorary doctorate from Union College (Mann, 1931, pp. 6, 7, 9, 12).

The overall goal of the IA involved four different elements ("Institute of Accountants and Book-keepers.," 1882b, pp. 189–190). One element was the promotion of the overall goal through "discussion . . . of technical knowledge and commercial practice" ("Institute of Accountants and Book-keepers.," 1882b, p. 189). This element primarily involved "lectures" delivered or "discussion[s]" held at IA meetings (see Cady, 1891, p. 189; also see, e.g., Romeo and Kyj, 1998, pp. 45–46, 51–55). Romeo and Kyj (1998, pp. 51–55) provide a list of such lectures and discussions. Lectures delivered at IA meetings as an educational strategy were consistent with public lectures, which for many communities in the U.S. for part of the nineteenth century were an important means of imparting knowledge (Scott, 1983). Another element was providing assistance to "members in their professional and social responsibilities" ("Institute of Accountants and Book-keepers.," 1882b, p. 189). This element likely was accomplished by members discussing with their colleagues about how to resolve challenging problems encountered in practice. An additional element was the provision of greater economic opportunities for members by vouching for the good character and competency for members in search of employment ("Institute of Accountants and Book-keepers.," 1882b, p. 189). Article 56 of the IA's by-laws mandated that the secretary maintain a record open to prospective employers that contained both resume types of information and examples of writing of members in need of employment ("Institute of Accountants and Book-keepers.," 1882b, p. 192). The final element was making available voluntary "Mutual Life Insurance [for] its members" ("Institute of Accountants and Book-keepers.," 1882b, pp. 189–190).

Association membership

The IA initially had two categories of membership, "Active" and "Honorary" ("Institute of Accountants and Book-keepers.," 1882b, p. 190). An initiation fee of "five dollars" and annual dues of "six dollars" for active members was sufficiently low to be affordable by many prospective candidates and all candidates for active membership were required to have "good moral character" and have "had practical experience as a double-entry book-keeper, and [be] qualified in the art of keeping accounts" ("Institute of Accountants and Book-keepers.," 1882b, p. 190). Active members also had had to pass an oral examination administered by a committee "of five members" ("Institute of Accountants and Book-keepers.,"

1882b, p. 192; also see "Favoring a National Institute.," 1883, pp. 293–294). This latter requirement, however, apparently could be waived or at least kept to a minimum for those known to have strong ethics and "experience and knowledge" in the discipline ("Institute of Accountants and Book-keepers.," 1882b, p. 192; also see "Examination for Membership in the Institute.," 1882, p. 338; Romeo and Kyj, 1998, pp. 36–37). The qualifying oral examination was not standardized and was characterized by one writer as a "social [chat]" that was "pleasant" ("Favoring a National Institute.," 1883, p. 294; also see the discussion in Romeo and Kyj, 1998, pp. 36–37). An honorary member (who had few associational rights) had to evidence "good moral standing," pay a $50 fee, and then when elected to membership apparently had to pay the $5 initiation fee and the annual $6 dues ("Institute of Accountants and Book-keepers.," 1882b, p. 190). We have not located any indication as to whether an applicant for honorary membership had to pass an examination. However, it seems unlikely since the requirements for such membership only mentioned good moral standing. Furthermore, we have not been able to locate any information as to whether anyone applied for honorary membership in the IA or was admitted as an honorary member. Members could receive "a Certificate of Membership" ("Institute of Accountants and Book-keepers.," 1882b, p. 192).

In what appears to have been May of 1886 the possibility of a different scheme of "grades" of "membership" and the issuance of "certificates" was raised at "the regular monthly meeting of the" IA ("The May Meeting.," 1886, p. 12). At that meeting the issue was sent "to the Executive Council for consideration and a report on the expediency of the measure" ("The May Meeting.," 1886, p. 12). A "special committee" to consider the issuing of "certificates and diplomas" was appointed in October of 1886 ("Institute of Accounts.," 1886b, p. 104). Such certificates and diplomas likely were meant to have more status than the Certificate of Membership initially authorized by the IA's by-laws (see "Institute of Accountants and Book-keepers.," 1882b, p. 192).

The special committee appears to have made its report at the January 15, 1887 meeting of the IA ("The Institute of Accounts.," 1887, p. 29). The committee recommended three classes of membership and proposed that one of the classes ("'Fellows'") could receive a "'certificate'" ("The Institute of Accounts.," 1887, p. 29). Also, it was recommended that the "honorary membership [be] abolished." ("The Institute of Accounts.," 1887, p. 29). The new proposed membership classes were then to be voted on at the February 1887 meeting of the IA ("The Institute of Accounts.," 1887, p. 29). At the February 15, 1887 meeting of the IA, the association adopted, with apparently some minor modifications, the proposal for the three new classes of membership as its membership categories ("Institute of Accounts, New York.," 1887, p. 51).

A notice in the January 1888 issue of *The Office: A Practical Journal of Business Management, Office Routine and the Art of Advertising* gave the following descriptions of these membership classes:

> The Institute is composed of three grades, viz.: Associates, Members and Fellows. Associates are admitted upon presentation of satisfactory credentials as to character and standing. Members are admitted after having appeared before the Committee on Membership and given evidence of satisfactory qualifications. Fellows (F.I.A.) are those Members who, having passed a satisfactory examination before the Board of Examination of the Fellows, are recommended to the Institute for the Degree.
>
> ("Institute of Accounts.," 1888a, p. vi)

Thus, individuals admitted as fellows apparently could use the initials F.I.A. "Fellow of the Institute of Accounts," ("Institute of Accounts.," 1888b, p. 49). In 1888 the "division" of the IA that administered the F.I.A. degree appears to have been called the "College of Fellows" ("Institute of Accounts.," 1888b, p. 48). The application procedures for becoming an F.I.A. are described in "Institute of Accounts." (1888b, pp. 48–49) and these procedures and the procedures noted in "Institute of Accounts." (1889, p. 138) suggest that not all applicants actually took a formal examination. These classifications in part may have been a reaction to the founding of the AAPA in 1886 (see note 6 and Figure 1.1) and that association's early efforts to enable its members to be able to use occupational related letters professionally (see Webster, 1954, pp. 64–66). Webster (1954, see pp. 65–66) quotes the AAPA's "1888 edition of the By-Laws" (p. 65) which notes that "'. . . members shall be divided into classes, styled respectively Fellows and Associates; the fellows to have the right to use the letters F.A.A., and the associates to have the right to use the letters A.A.A., to designate their degrees of membership respectively'" (p. 66).

By the 1890s the IA's member classifications eventually proved unsatisfactory, most likely to its membership in public practice. This dissatisfaction was likely partially due to the competitive practice environment that the latter echelon began to experience early in the 1890s from the influx of immigrant British practitioners who belonged to the highly prestigious Institute of Chartered Accountants of England and Wales (Miranti, 1988, p. 362; also see the discussion in Miranti, 1990, pp. 45–46). Also, as we discuss later, in the early part of the 1890s the AAPA promoted a plan for controlling entrance to public accounting by establishing a "College of Accounts."

Thus, by 1895, the IA had reformed its membership classes (see "Progressive Accounting," 1895). More specifically, the IA had a three-tiered membership hierarchy based on experience and on successful completion of qualifying examinations. The categories were: "Associates," "Certified Accountants," and "Fellows" ("Progressive Accounting," 1895). Associates were "admitted upon presentation of satisfactory credentials as to character, etc., and are entitled to all the privileges of the Institute, except voting and holding office" ("Progressive Accounting," 1895). Certified Accountants were "members" with "practical experience as double entry bookkeepers who successfully pass . . . an examination in technical accounting and business practice . . ." and were allowed to place the letters

"*C.A.* after their names while members of the Institute" ("Progressive Accounting," 1895). Fellows of the Institute signified their status through use of the abbreviation "*F.I.A.*," and included only those who had served as "Certified Accountants" for at least "one year" and had passed another "examination" that was "prescribed by an examining Board of Fellows" ("Progressive Accounting," 1895). Also, "formal certificates [were] issued to Certified Accountants and Fellows" ("Progressive Accounting," 1895). The use of these qualifying initials heightened tensions within the local New York City practitioner community because of their similarity with those used by chartered accountants (see Romeo and Kyj, 1998, p. 41).

Professional characteristics

Ethical norms

The IA, like many emerging professional groups, was also sensitive to the need to establish an ethical framework to provide assurances that its members would apply their professional knowledge only in ways that would benefit the interests of society (see, e.g., the general discussion in Caplow, 1954, p. 139 and Wilensky, 1964, pp. 138, 140–141, 145–146). Although we have not found a code of ethics, the IA's commitment seems to have been expressed more generally through such requirements (as noted above) that all applying to become an active member be of "good moral character" ("good moral standing" in the case of someone wishing to become an honorary member) ("Institute of Accountants and Bookkeepers.," 1882b, p. 190). Also, the IA could try and sanction members found guilty of "any offense calculated to bring disrepute upon the Institute" ("Institute of Accountants and Bookkeepers.," 1882b, p. 192).

The moral intent of the IA was also reflected both in its seal, which employed a triangular design, and also its motto. A depiction of what was likely all or part of the seal is presented in Figure 2.1 and was said to mean "'Knowledge and Experience uniting on a base of Integrity, and pointing

Figure 2.1 The probable seal of the Institute of Accounts.

Source: Reproduced from "The Institute of Accounts" (1894, p. 184). As discussed in the text, the reproduction depicts what was probably all or part of the Institute of Accounts' seal.

upward'" ("The Institute of Accounts," 1894, p. 184; also see Romeo and Kyj, 1998, p. 35). The quotation in the previous sentence is also identified as the "'motto'" of the IA and that quotation is attributed to a letter written by J.H. McNish that was read apparently after a dinner the IA held on 15 May 1894 at a hotel "across the street" from the IA's "rooms" and also was published in part in the May 1894 issue of *Business: A Practical Journal of the Office* ("The Institute of Accounts," 1894, p. 184; also see Romeo and Kyj, 1998, p. 35).[7] The dinner had followed a business meeting at the IA's rooms at which newly elected officers were installed ("The Institute of Accounts," 1894, p. 184). At the business meeting that preceded the dinner, Frederick W. Child, the IA's new president, gave an "inaugural address" in which he noted that "'the words inscribed on the seal of this Institute, "Knowledge, Experience and Integrity," represent the three most requisite qualifications of a successful accountant'" ("The Institute of Accounts," 1894, p. 184). An article in the September 1899 issue of *Accountics: The Office Magazine* mentions that the IA had an "emblem" and the discussion in the article raises the possibility that the IA's seal may have been enclosed by "a circle" (see "Hartford Chapter of the Institute of Accounts," 1899, p. 53).

Education

Another aspect of the IA involvement in the promotion of knowledge found expression through its sponsorship of "lectures, discussion, comparisons of data and direct instruction" at its meetings (Cady, 1891, p. 189; also see, e.g., Romeo and Kyj, 1998, pp. 45–46, 51–55) and at some point its establishment of a library. Initially the meetings of the IA were held "at 29 Warren Street" ("First Fall Meeting of the Institute.," 1882, p. 302) which was also the address of offices of *The Book-Keeper* (see, e.g., "*Advertisement of 'The Book-Keeper.',*" 1882, p. 315). By 1886 the IA shifted the focus of these activities to the "University Building, Washington Square, East" ("Institute of Accounts.," 1886a, p. 84; also see "Institute of Accounts.," 1891, p. 238). Although we are not aware of any record of the holdings of the IA's library, evidence indicates that this resource was established by 1893 (see Figure 2.2) when the IA had its headquarters at "98 Fifth avenue" ("The Institute of Accounts," 1893, p. 321). The picture in Figure 2.2 does not show shelves on which there are books. There does appear to be books on at least one table in the picture. In 1897 the New York chapter of the IA appears to have had offices at "144 Madison avenue" ("New York Chapter," 1897, p. 14).

VIEW IN THE LIBRARY OF THE INSTITUTE OF ACCOUNTS, NEW YORK

Figure 2.2 The Institute of Accounts' library *circa* 1893.

Source: The picture is reproduced from "The Institute of Accounts" (1893, p. 321). The caption under the picture stating, "VIEW IN THE LIBRARY OF THE INSTITUTE OF ACCOUNTS, NEW YORK," is also reproduced from "The Institute of Accounts" (1893, p. 321) where it is a caption under the picture. Also, see the discussion in "The Institute of Accounts" (1893, p. 321).

Nationwide scope

Although early in the IA's existence its leaders aspired to establish a national scope for the IA (see, e.g., "A National Institute of Accountants," 1883, pp. 37–38), these efforts were only modestly successful. An Institute of Accountants and Book-keepers of Chicago, apparently in some way tied to the IA, was founded in Chicago during 1883 ("Institute News.," 1883, pp. 154–155). The Institute of Accountants and Book-keepers of Chicago apparently did not thrive (see McMillan, 1998b,

p. 75), being somehow displaced by the 1890s by such organizations as the Chicago Society of Accountants (e.g., "Chicago
Society of Accountants," 1897, p. 143), the Illinois Society of
Public Accountants (Miranti, 1990, p. 61; Reckitt, 1940,
p. 379), and apparently for a brief time by the Illinois Institute
of Accounts–Chicago ("The Institute of Accounts," 1897;
"Official Roster of Accountants' Associations," 1897a, 1897b).

A major drive to expand the IA's geographic scope throughout the U.S. was mounted in 1897 after the passage of New
York CPA law at which time the IA became "a Federation of
Chapters" ("Nationalization of the Institute of Accounts,"
1897, p. 14). The new entity had members in various locations
in the U.S. in which there were no IA chapters, such as New
Orleans, Pittsburgh, San Francisco, and Texas ("Convention of
the Institute of Accounts," 1897, p. 66; "John W. Amermann.
M.I.A.," 1897, p. 99). However, permanent chapters emerged
in at least New York City, Massachusetts, Hartford (Connecticut), and Washington, D.C. ("New York Accountants' Headquarters," 1897, p. 82; "Nationalization of the Institute of
Accounts," 1897, p. 14; "Massachusetts Institute of Accounts,"
1897, p. 67; "Washington Chapter of the Institute of
Accounts," 1898, p. 93; "Hartford Chapter," 1898a, p. 124;
1898b, pp. 3–6). Also, for a short period of time there may
have been a chapter in Chicago called the Illinois Institute of
Accounts–Chicago ("The Institute of Accounts," 1897;
"Official Roster of Accountants' Associations," 1897a, 1897b).

A note in the July 1898 issue of *Accountics: The Office
Magazine* discusses a presentation made by A.O. Kittredge to
the Illinois Institute of Accountants "in the office of the Illinois
Steel Company, Chicago" in July of 1898 ("Illinois Institute of
Accountants," 1898, p. 89). This latter organization "was
incorporated in 1896" and does not appear to have been a
chapter of the IA ("Illinois Institute of Accountants," 1899,
pp. 89–90). While efforts were made to start a chapter in
Brooklyn (N.Y.) ("Brooklyn Chapter," 1898a, p. 124; 1898b,
p. 45), we have not found any evidence that a Brooklyn chapter
was established. Also, a note in *Accountics: A Monthly*

Magazine for Office Men indicated, "active steps are being taken by certain members of the Bookkeepers' Beneficial Association of Philadelphia towards the formation of the Philadelphia Chapter of the Institute of Accounts" ("A Philadelphia Chapter," 1897, p. 15). We have found no evidence of the establishment of a chapter in Philadelphia. Also, while there are indications that in 1897 the IA had hoped to establish chapters in additional cities (see, e.g., "The Institute of Accounts," 1897, p. 54; also see Webster, 1954, p. 281), we have not located evidence of any other such chapters.

Besides the New York chapter, the only chapter that seemed to thrive, however, was the Hartford chapter, which appears to have had some members who were from the city's business community (see, e.g., "Hartford Chapter," 1898b, pp. 3–4; "Hartford Chapter of Institute of Accounts," 1899, pp. 52–53). A note in *Accountics: The Office Magazine* in August of 1900 indicated that *Accountics: The Office Magazine* was still the "Official Journal" of "The Hartford Chapter of the Institute of Accounts" ("*Accountics: The Office Magazine*," 1900b, p. 23). However, we have not been able to locate later information about the IA's Hartford chapter.

Evidence suggests that the Massachusetts chapter did not survive beyond 1897 or perhaps 1898.[8] The Washington, D.C. chapter was formed in January of 1898 ("Washington Chapter of the Institute of Accounts," 1898, p. 93). An account of the "annual convention" of the IA in June of 1900 suggests that the Washington, D.C. chapter was still in existence ("Convention of the Institute of Accounts," 1900, p. 88) and a note in *Accountics: The Office Magazine* in August of 1900 indicated that *Accountics: The Office Magazine* was still the "Official Journal" of "The Washington Chapter of the Institute of Accounts" ("*Accountics: The Office Magazine*," 1900b, p. 23). However, we have not been able to locate later information about the IA's Washington, D.C. chapter.

After 1897 it is likely that many public accountants in the U.S. were more interested in joining associations more explicitly identified with the developing CPA movement. For example, it appears that the first accounting association organized in the State of Maryland had as its original principal purpose the passage of a CPA law (see, e.g., Wilkinson, 1903, p. 460; Loeb, 2002b, pp. 10–13). Thus, it may have been difficult for the IA to establish a new chapter or, when new chapters were established, for the chapters to survive.

Publications

The IA also disseminated information about its affairs and knowledge of accounting matters through a series of publications published by two founding members, Selden R. Hopkins and Anson O. Kittredge, who both originally hailed from Ohio (Webster, 1954, pp. 108–109). Hopkins had begun his career as a bookkeeper in Milwaukee in 1860 and made the transition to public practice in 1868 after intervening Union Army service in the Civil War and service as a commercial school principal (Webster, 1954, p. 108). In 1879 he authored a book on bookkeeping, which was later adopted for courses at the Wharton School of the University of Pennsylvania (Webster, 1954, p. 108). Between 1879 and 1896 Hopkins had an independent accounting practice in New York City and published three successive journals dealing with the problems of bookkeeping and office management (Webster, 1954, p. 108). He served as coeditor with Colonel Sprague on the earlier two, *The Bookkeeper* and *American Counting-room* (Webster, 1954, p. 108; The Committee on History, 1952, p. 431). His last publishing venture, however, *Treasury*, proved less successful, running at least five issues before folding, likely in 1885 (Webster, 1954, p. 108).

The publications launched by Anson Kittredge reflected the editorial skills of one who brought to the task both knowledge of accounting and over a decade's experience in business publishing. After graduation from Miami (Ohio) Commercial College and a brief stint as a clerk in a foundry, Kittredge gravitated to publishing in the mid-1870s, serving as editor on a metal industry trade journal and a building industry trade journal ("Anson O. Kittredge," 1903, pp. 9–10; Webster, 1954, p. 109; Romeo and Kyj, 2000, pp. 119–120).

In addition, in 1898 Kittredge founded and was president of a New York City accounting firm called the Accounting, Audit & Assurance Co. that was known for its systems expertise ("Anson O. Kittredge," 1903, p. 10). Kittredge was involved from 1886 to 1896 as editor and/or owner of *The Office* that was later rechristened *Business* ("Anson O. Kittredge," 1903, p. 10; Webster, 1954, p. 109; Romeo and Kyj, 2000, p. 120). He was also editor of *Accountics*, and as noted below, very likely editor of *Commerce, Accounts & Finance* (Webster, 1954, p. 109; also see Romeo and Kyj, 2000, p. 118). The journals with which Kittredge was involved were broader in scope than Hopkins's, covering general business conditions, accounting, and office management problems, and the activities of many business and professional societies (also see the discussion in Romeo and Kyj, 2000, pp. 121–122, 136). Although the IA's affairs were an important topic in the first two of these publications, *Accountics* was the only one that claimed to function as "the official publication of the" IA (when the IA became a national organization) and at that time to also be the "Official Journal" of "The New York Chapter of the Institute of Accounts" ("Official Journal," 1897, p. 16; also see Romeo and Kyj, 2000, p. 121). *Accountics* eventually became the "Official Journal" of the IA's Washington, D.C. and Hartford, Connecticut chapters (e.g., "*Accountics: The Office Magazine*," 1900a, p. 7).

Commerce, Accounts & Finance, which listed George E. Allen and Joseph Crosby Lincoln as editors, on the other hand, became closely identified with New York University's (NYU's) School of Commerce, Accounts, and Finance (SCAF), an institution Kittredge served as a "professor of the theory and practice of accounts" ("Anson O. Kittredge," 1903, p. 10). Kittredge served as the business manager of *Commerce, Accounts & Finance*. His likely editorial influence on that journal is evidenced by the cessation of the publication of that journal within two months of Anson Kittredge's death in March 1903 (see Webster, 1954, p. 109).

3 Functionality of the IA and its role in professionalization

Problems facing bookkeeping in the U.S. in the late nineteenth century

The professional programs that the IA promoted were appealing to many bookkeepers because they were responsive to serious problems associated with working as a bookkeeper. Many of the IA's bookkeepers were likely concerned about their marginal economic status (see the discussion in "Compensation vs. Services," 1881, pp. 136–137). Bookkeepers, for example, likely were sensitive to their relative low rate of pay as compared to other business specialists such as salesmen ("Compensation vs. Services," 1881, pp. 136–137). Thus, bookkeepers were vulnerable to destitution should they become unemployed. A sensitivity to this insecurity was reflected in the above-noted goals of establishing life insurance and employment referral services (also see Webster, 1954, p. 12).

A second problem was the marginal image of bookkeepers as sources of authority in accounting matters. This lack of authority was largely a function of the limited educational infrastructure available to prepare and certify candidates' fitness for professional accounting careers. Unlike the situation in law, engineering, and medicine (see the discussion in Collins, 1979, pp. 141–142, 150–155, 163–171; Calvert, 1967, chapters 3–5; McMillan, 1998b, pp. 118–119), little had been done to forge strong connections between accounting and the country's emerging colleges and universities. Moreover, the problems of pedagogy were made more difficult by the lack of a well-defined theoretical framework for guiding the evolution of practice, as was common in other learned callings, a deficiency that, as we shall see in the following Section, IA leaders tried diligently to cure. Many, consequently, received their training in classes at proprietary business academies that in some instances may have provided rote instruction (see the discussion in McMillan, 1998b, pp. 112–113). One IA leader, Silas S. Packard, operated a proprietary business school located in New York City (see, e.g., "Packard, Silas Sadler," 1893; "Silas S. Packard," 1898; McMillan, 1998b, p. 117). Others likely relied on practical experience gained while working in a counting room, which was perhaps augmented by self study (see the general discussion in McMillan, 1998b, pp. 110–112).

During this era collegiate business education was in its infancy, led by the innovative Wharton School in the 1880s (see the discussion in Sass, 1982, chapter 2; Miranti, 1988, pp. 366–367; 1990, pp. 40–41) and later, after October 1, 1900, also by NYU's SCAF (Miranti, 1990, pp. 42–43; Committee on History, 1953b, p. 262). Both of these schools are discussed later. Because of these circumstances, a number of bookkeepers likely had limited competency and were capable of handling only the routine transaction processing of simple, small businesses. Their formal training likely did little to prepare them to think creatively about measuring the new economic processes of great scale and complexity, which were rapidly transforming the nation's business sector (see the general discussion in Herrick, 1923, pp. 91–96 and Miranti, 1990, p. 39).

The personal backgrounds of the first leadership cadre of the IA suggest that most were employees of prosperous firms (see "Edward C. Cockey," 1883; also see note 9). Moreover, these individuals were not just clerks but, instead, exercised important supervisory authority in their respective businesses (see "Edward C. Cockey," 1883; also see note 9). For example, the

Institute's first president, Edward C. Cockey, a descendant of one of Maryland's early, leading families ("Edward C. Cockey," 1883, p. 33), first learned bookkeeping while working in his father's mercantile business in Baltimore and later honed these skills during the Civil War when he was "in charge of" accounting for the Union Army's "Ordinance Department" "at Fortress Monroe" ("Edward C. Cockey," 1883, p. 34). After the war he moved to New York and at the formation of the IA was "storekeeper of the Western Union Telegraph Company, in New York City" ("Edward C. Cockey," 1883, p. 33; also see p. 34).[9]

Value of IA programs in dealing with professional problems

The programs for professionalization sponsored by the IA created an image of accountants and bookkeepers as agents of "progress" (see "The Institute of Accounts," 1894, p. 184; also see the general discussion in "Progressive Accounting," 1895) and social uplift that helped to counter a more negative perception conveyed through popular literature in such works as Charles Dickens's classic, *A Christmas Carol*.[10] In addition to providing the accounting occupation with a progressive image, as discussed later, the IA, for its first 15 years, served as a catalyst for professional progress and progressive professional change. The IA's activities were also meaningful for some members of the business community (see note 26). Contact with Silas Packard through the auspices of the IA doubtless provided members of the business community with opportunities to elicit referrals of promising students who might be recruited (see the discussion in Miranti, 1990, pp. 38–39). In addition, the IA's meetings likely became useful venues for identifying experts who could be engaged for consultation about the best ways to resolve thorny accounting problems or to design more effective reporting systems (see the general discussion in "Progressive Accounting," 1895, especially the section on the "Advantages of Membership"). The IA's meetings, as we shall see in the following section, were also valuable in communicating new ideas about accounting theory and practice.

Although education was a key purpose of the IA, few members likely devoted themselves fully to pedagogical pursuits. The one notable exception was Silas Packard for whom the IA likely was an important contact point with both public accountants and other individuals in the business community who might hire individuals graduating from his academy (see Miranti, 1990, p. 39). In addition, the IA's meetings likely provided opportunities for eliciting information about the adequacy of his academy's "curriculum" (see Miranti, 1990, p. 39; also see p. 38). Lastly, Packard also likely drew close to the IA when, as we shall see, a rival professional body, the AAPA, established a school in 1893. The subsequent involvement of several prominent IA members in the promotion of collegiate accounting education, however, suggests the possibility that some IA members may have perceived that existing proprietary academies and the IA's educational programs had limitations in providing training for accounting novices.[11]

The usefulness of the IA to the fledgling public accounting occupation

The involvement of public accountants in the affairs of the IA, on the other hand, likely was conditioned by a more complex set of motives. The interest of public accountants in the IA often complemented those of IA members not in public accounting. The IA, for example, undoubtedly provided public accountants with a useful forum for making contact with prospective clients and for demonstrating their virtuosity in some aspect of practice through activities such as lecturing. Additionally, the organization's meetings probably served as contact points for the recruitment of promising junior accountants.[12]

But the forces of economic change were creating new opportunities for the public accountants (see, e.g., the general discussion in Galambos and Pratt, 1988, pp. 1–37). The range of services provided by the infant public accounting profession in the U.S. expanded significantly by the 1890s. Some practitioners established reputations for specialties, as did William Bainbridge Jaudon of New York City who "made a specialty of accounting in the Surrogate's Court ..." ("William Bainbridge Jaudon," 1897, p. 47). This involved work relating to settling the estates of decendents (see Jaudon, 1897, p. 27). Charles Dutton "made a specialty of the adjustment of accounts in litigation and of municipal examinations" ("Charles Dutton," 1897, p. 20). Anson Kittredge was known for developing efficient accounting systems for client entities ("Anson O. Kittredge," 1903, p. 10).

The take-off period for accountant's certification services, however, did not arise in the U.S. until the increase in industrial mergers at the end of the nineteenth and the beginning of the twentieth centuries (see the discussion in Miranti, 1990, p. 49; Allen and McDermott, 1993, pp. 3, 19–21; Lamoreaux, 1985, chapter 1; Wilkins, 1989, pp. 542–543). Earlier, the financial reporting by the nation's first big business, the railroads, had been largely controlled by the Interstate Commerce Commission, which provided few opportunities for public accountants. Under the Interstate Commerce Act (1887) independent public accountants were not made responsible for certifying to the accuracy of the information in corporate filings with the federal government (Miranti, 1990, p. 32; also see, e.g., Miranti, 1989, p. 471; Smykay, 1955, p. 2). The formation of great industrial organizations in the latter part of the nineteenth century (see, e.g., the discussion in Galambos and Pratt, 1988, pp. 28–37), however, helped breathe new life into the market for public accountant certification (e.g., see the discussion in Allen and McDermott, 1993, pp. 3, 19–21; Reckitt, 1953, pp. 30–32; Wilkins, 1989, pp. 536–546). But there was also a concern that the disclosures provided by industrial organizations were simply too meager to protect the investing public ("'Men Loved Darkness Rather Than Light, For Their Deeds Were Evil.'," 1901, p. 1).

In the next Section, our focus shifts to concern with the nature of accounting knowledge.

4 The structure of accounting knowledge and the natural order of society

A central feature in the IA's program of professionalism was the definition of the knowledge base of accounting in the form of an intellectual construct known both as "accountics" and the "science of accountancy." This system of ideas had, as we shall show in this section, at least four functions that included: (A) making comprehensible the basic organization of accounting knowledge and the use of measurement and classifications through which the benefits of such knowledge were channeled to society; (B) clarifying the relationship of the knowledge base and occupational segments; (C) developing the knowledge base including the areas of account classification, analytical techniques, systems, and auditing; and (D) searching for ways accounting could serve government and business leaders in addressing problems to more effectively order society. These concepts had been developing for some time before the IA had been founded (see McMillan, 1998b, chapter 2; 1998c).

Accountics or the science of accounts

Although the term "accountics" was likely first defined in 1887 by Colonel Charles Sprague in lectures at "the School of Library Economy at Columbia College" ("Mathematical Elucidation of Accounts.," 1887, p. 103; also see McMillan, 1998b, p. 44; 1998c, pp. 18–19), many of the key notions supporting his vision had already been crystallized seven years earlier in his classic essay, "The Algebra of Accounts" (Sprague, 1880a, pp. 2–4, 19–22, 34–35, 44–48, 51–53; also see McMillan, 1998b, p. 44; 1998c, p. 19). In a synopsis of the lectures reported in *The Office*, the term "accountics" was considered to be a "mathematical science of values" ("Mathematical Elucidation of Accounts.," 1887, p. 103; see also McMillan, 1998b, pp. 44–45; 1998c, pp. 19–20). By stressing its mathematical properties, Sprague drew accounting closer to the mainstream in nineteenth-century economic thought that took inspiration from (1) the ancient thought of the Pythagoreans and (2) the later system of Newtonian physics, both of which embodied a central belief in a precisely ordered universe (see the discussion in Guthrie, 1971, pp. 212–226 and Cohen, 1994).[13]

Besides emulating the example of economics, the tools of mathematical science doubtless seemed superior to Sprague because of the greater intellectual flexibility it afforded over the mechanical rubrics that hitherto had been the primary ways for elucidating accounting (see the discussion in McMillan, 1998b, pp. 45–47; 1998c, pp. 20–22). The primary advantage of mathematics was its implicit precision, which, when applied in the evaluation of other forms of knowledge, made possible the exact specification of key interrelationships. This Sprague ably demonstrated in accounting by equating algebraically the relationship between assets, liabilities, and equity on the balance sheet in "The Algebra of Accounts" (Sprague, 1880a, pp. 2–4, 19–22, 34–35, 44–48, 51–53). In addition, measurement assisted by a system of account classification that accurately reflected economic realities made possible the exercise of control over phenomena that otherwise seemed unordered (see McMillan, 1998b, chapter 2, especially p. 45, and the discussion on pp. 50–52; 1998c, especially p. 20 and the discussion on pp. 25–27). And by reducing accounting to mathematical expression the potential was also created for establishing stronger intellectual bridges to other forms of knowledge – physical, social, and even moral – that were susceptible to quantification (see the discussion in McMillan, 1998b, chapter 2, especially pp. 34–37, 41–50; 1998c, especially, pp. 10–13, 16–25).

Knowledge base and occupational segments

In 1897, the year after the passage of the New York CPA law (which is discussed later), the notions of accountics or the science of accounts were amplified and used to explain and justify the emerging differentiation between roles of various parts of the accounting community, an ongoing process that attempted to distinguish between the true expert from the mere technician. More specifically, Charles Dutton, a public accountant ("Charles Dutton, F.I.A.," 1897, p. 20) and in April of that year president of the New York chapter of the IA ("New York Chapter," 1897, p. 14), tried to provide insight into this pattern of change by advancing a simple triune conception of accountics (Dutton, 1897, p. 4). The first component was accounting, which was conceived as "an element of business" and was thought essential for making comprehensible complex economic processes and for achieving "harmonious relations" between interdependent business enterprises (Dutton, 1897, pp. 3–5). The second element of accountics was the "Science of Accounts" ("a knowledge of the expression or manifestation of accounting") whose "exponent," [the] professional "Accountant," was responsible for analytical application of accounting knowledge to determine the correctness of records, to search for causal explanations, and to conduct inquiries as to the most effective methods for applying knowledge (Dutton, 1897, p. 4). The third was "the Art of Bookkeeping" whose "exponent," "the Bookkeeper," was viewed as an artist involved in the "synthetical" application of knowledge to synthesize information about business affairs (Dutton, 1897, p. 4).

Four years later, in 1901, Charles Sprague put forth a different definition of the general principles constituting accountics in an article based upon his "lectures" (1901, p. 3) at NYU's SCAF. While also stressing knowledge hierarchies and functional specialization, Sprague's position in these lectures differed from that of Dutton by directly equating the science of accounts with accountics (Sprague, 1901, pp. 3–4). In Sprague's view accountics or the science of accounts was synonymous and dedicated to realizing two goals in business affairs: "information" and "protection" (Sprague, 1901, p. 4). He (1901, pp. 4–5) suggested that information was the use of accounting data and systems to assist business decision processes. Sprague (1901, p. 5) further suggested that protection was concerned with using accounting data and systems to prevent the loss of enterprise resources both internally and externally.

Sprague believed that the transmission of the science of accounts to the business world depended on the actions of practitioners of five "kindred arts": "bookkeeping," "auditing," "accountancy," "system-building," and "business management" (Sprague, 1901, p. 3). The bookkeeper was responsible for "the keeping of accounts" but was thought to lack the creativity inherent in the role of the "skilled accountant" (see Sprague, 1901, p. 3). Using a mechanical analogy, Sprague contrasted bookkeepers and accountants:

> The difference between the person who keeps accounts skillfully and the skilled accountant who understands his science is like the difference between the skillful engineer who can run a complicated engine . . . and the mechanician who is able to build that engine, or repair it, or take it to pieces, or, when necessary, invent another one for special purposes.
>
> (Sprague, 1901, p. 3)

The "second art," auditing, on the other hand, was a higher order activity involving "the power of criticising the work of the bookkeeper" (Sprague, 1901, p. 3). The third art, accountancy, concentrated on "the interpretation of" the significance of the information compiled by bookkeepers (Sprague, 1901, p. 3). Sprague used the analogy of the historian and the diarist to further distinguish the activities of the practitioner of accountancy from that of bookkeeper. Like the diarist, the bookkeeper specialized in recording "details of facts," while the accountant uses this information to create "a history of a certain business ... and show ... what has been done, and wherein it has succeeded and wherein it has failed" (Sprague, 1901, p. 3). The fourth art, "system-building" or "systematology," represented a more challenging application of accounting knowledge practiced only by the more astute practitioners (Sprague, 1901, p. 3). More specifically, Sprague (1901, p. 3) noted that this specialization "as we rise higher in the sphere, becomes confined to fewer persons, and is still more important and of higher utility – the power to construct system of accounts for special purposes, for any purpose that may be required, from the humblest commercial enterprise to the accounts of the United States Treasury." And lastly all of these previously noted functions, which were designed to protect and to inform, were conceived as vital adjuncts to the process of managing a business organization (Sprague, 1901, p. 3; also see pp. 4–5).

IA's role in developing a knowledge base

Besides adumbrating the broad outlines of accountics, the IA's leaders were deeply concerned about illuminating specific questions of accounting theory and practice. The growing information requirements of a more complex economic order motivated efforts to search for underlying principles for standardizing accounting. Such a search was valuable because it reduced the growing asymmetric distribution of information between investors and business managers (see Baskin and Miranti, 1997, chapter 5).

The need for more reliable and comprehensive financial information likely was first addressed in the U.S. by the railroads, the nation's initial large industry, which was considering such issues in the decade of the 1850s (see Chandler, 1977, pp. 109–121; Miranti, 1989, p. 471; also see the general discussion in Brief, 1965, pp. 14–17). Accounting standardization was later advanced by state and federal regulators of railroads and other monopolistic industries who desired greater transparency of corporate affairs to monitor rate regulatory compliance and to inform investors (see the discussion in Miranti, 1989, pp. 469–493, 503–509; 1990, pp. 89–94; Smykay, 1955, chapters 1–3). However, notwithstanding such governmental involvement with accounting standardization for regulated industries, there were many conceptual and theoretical accounting issues for private groups such as the IA to consider.

In the debates over the conceptual and theoretical bases for accounting, Sprague again played a leading role, a commitment that doubtless grew out of a deep and abiding personal interest in improving the efficiency of many forms of communication. An early member of the Modern Language Association, the Colonel had been a proponent of a more simple phonetic way to spell espoused by a pioneer of library science, Melvil Dewey. Sprague was also a proponent of Volapuk, an international language (Miranti, 1988, p. 367; 1990, pp. 38, 50, 203; 1993a, p. viii; 1996, p. 15; The Committee on History, 1952, p. 430; Mann, 1931, pp. 42–44). In addition, he "[devoted] time to the development of bookkeeping and office machinery..." (Miranti, 1990, p. 38). In providing illumination about the nature of accounting knowledge, Sprague and his colleagues in the IA, as we shall discuss in the following sections, focused a good deal of their writing and lecturing on four related issues: (1) the classification of accounts, (2) analytical aids to practice, (3) systems development, and (4) auditing.

Account classification

A key concern confronting Sprague and IA colleagues was that of account classification, a vital process enabling accounting to interface with the allied fields of law (see the general discussion in both Clarke, 1902 and Gordon, 1983) and economics (see the discussion in Johnson, 1902). The central issue involved the definition of concepts and a technical vocabulary useful in structuring accounts so that they accurately reflected the legal and economic realities that affected the enterprise and its stakeholders (see the discussion in McMillan, 1998b, pp. 21–22, 23–54; 1998c).

Commercial law defined stakeholder relationships that eventually supported the early formulation of the proprietary theory of accounting by Sprague in his paradigmatic essay, "The Algebra of Accounts" (1880a, pp. 2–4, 19–22, 34–35, 44–48, 51–53). Sprague's (1880a) model was consistent with the business organizations that characterized a number of firms in the U.S. during the nineteenth century (see the discussion in Chandler, 1977, pp. 33–50; Baskin and Miranti, 1997, chapter 4; Galambos and Pratt, 1988, pp. 17–28). Although accountants debated the precise definition of liabilities and equity ("'Debit' and 'Credit'," 1882, pp. 381–383; "'Is Capital Account a Liability?'," 1882, pp. 397–398), the status of creditors and owners described by Sprague in his "Algebra of Accounts" (1880a, e.g., pp. 2–3, 19–22) and later refined in *The Philosophy of Accounts* (1907) provided useful measures of financing sources in small, non-complex businesses (see the discussion in Sprague, 1907, chapters 4, 5, 7, 8). Problems encountered in providing professional services to clients organized as partnerships were the subject of correspondence in *The Book-Keeper* (see, e.g., Clemens, 1882; Corning, 1882). The emerging proprietary model also influenced the accounting for corporations, a business form whose use in business was on the upswing in the 1880s (see "Joint-Stock Book-keeping.," 1881, p. 113; "Changing from a Partnership to a Corporation.," 1883; also see the discussion in Chatfield, 1974, pp. 220–225). As in the case of partnerships, problems encountered in corporate accounting were at times addressed through correspondence in *The Book-Keeper* as to the best practice for resolving particular problems (see, for example, "Technical Discussions," 1882, pp. 213–214, 293).

A major problem in economic science, or for that matter any formal body of knowledge, then as well as now, is the development of classifications that can accommodate items with seemingly dissimilar attributes. Thus, the articles and debates of the IA's leading luminaries grappled with such quandaries as differing temporal aspects of balance sheet and profit and loss accounts, the connections between outlays and the revenue earning process, and the character of liability and equity accounts ("'Is Capital Account a Liability?'," 1882; Packard, 1884, pp. 78–79; Sprague, 1889; also, see the discussion in Hopkins, 1883; McMillan, 1998b, pp. 33–50; 1998c, pp. 8–25).

In addition, accountants could keep abreast of developments in law by reading reprinted articles from other specialized magazines. Synopses of legal decisions from *Bradstreet's*, for example, frequently appeared in *The Book-Keeper* (see, e.g., "Decisions in Commercial Law," 1882). Later, *Commerce, Accounts & Finance* relied on Thomas B. Paton for reprinted articles from the *Banking Law Journal* on the law of negotiable instruments (Paton, 1902, 1903). Also, accounting-related journals in the later part of the nineteenth and the early twentieth century published articles relating to economics that may have had accompanying notes indicating that the article originated from another source or sources. For example, congressional testimony on the use of paper money appeared in the *American Counting-room* (Curtis, 1884).

Guidance for transaction measurement and statement presentation focused on problems that likely fell outside the scope of basic commercial practice addressed in proprietary school courses or bookkeeping textbooks. Some lectures and articles dealt with specialized businesses such as the unique accounting problems relating to "the Surrogate Court" (Jaudon, 1897, p. 27; also see pp. 28–35), municipal governments (Hopkins, 1883, 1884), savings banks ("Bank Book-Keeping.," 1880–1881) (which were published before the founding of the IA), and building and loan associations (Keys, 1884).

Analytical techniques

Analytic techniques involving the use of mathematics to discover errors or to determine balances were also useful in the late nineteenth century to a generation of bookkeepers and accountants whose formal education was unlikely to have been sufficient to qualify them for high school graduation.[14] One contributor to the literature on analytical practices was Joseph Hardcastle, who was born in Great Britain but ultimately emigrated to the U.S. (The Committee on History, 1951, p. 615). He had the benefit of an excellent education and had experience as both a teacher and a school administrator (The Committee on History, 1951, p. 615). It was likely that, due to his erudition, Hardcastle was selected to serve on the IA's examining committee (see "Institute of Accountants and Book-keepers.," 1882a, p. 173; also see Flesher *et al.*, 1996, p. 17). Hardcastle wrote about the problems of calculating interest and discounts (Hardcastle, 1883a, 1884, 1903a, 1903b), present value calculations (Hardcastle, 1883a, 1903a), and even, as the title indicates, "On the Theory of Life Insurance" (Hardcastle, 1883b). The use of analytical techniques was also of interest to Sprague who had written on the topic of using such techniques in discovering errors in the balance sheet (see Sprague, 1880b).

Systems development

The creation of accounting systems that were more "efficient" and effective in maintaining financial control was a cutting-edge activity that had distinguished some of the members of the IA (see the general discussion in McMillan, 1998a, 1998b, chapter 4). For example, as discussed later, Charles Waldo Haskins, who was drawn to the IA late in the 1890s, had worked, during President Cleveland's second administration (see Jordan, 1923, p. 17), with Elijah Watt Sells (who at a later time was to become his partner in the firm of Haskins & Sells), on "a joint commission of congress" ("Haskins, Charles Waldo," 1907, p. 515) whose recommendations, among other things, resulted in revisions to the "accounting system" (see, e.g., Jordan, 1923, pp. 39, 45) used by the U.S. Department of the Treasury (see, e.g., the discussion in Kraines, 1954, especially pp. 420–421, 430–440; Miranti, 1990, p. 36; Jordan, 1923, pp. 15–49; Skowronek, 1982, p. 50; Haskins & Sells, 1970, p. 12; McMillan, 1998a, pp. 129–134; 1998b, pp. 99–105). That commission viewed the revisions to the accounting system at the Department of the Treasury as a key accomplishment (Kraines, 1954, pp. 431–432). Hardcastle (see, e.g., 1888, 1889a, 1889b) considered issues relating to building and loan associations.

In addition, Colonel Sprague was likely the author of a series of articles on savings bank bookkeeping reported in *The Book-Keeper* ("Bank Book-Keeping.," 1880–1881). Hardcastle and Sprague also promoted public awareness of "logismography," an innovative system of accounting invented by Giuseppi Cerbini while "Accountant General of Italy" (Sprague, 1898a, p. 73, also see pp. 74–75; 1898b; Hardcastle, 1897a, 1897b, 1897c, 1897d, 1897e, 1897f; McMillan, 1998b, pp. 52–53; 1998c, p. 28). Kittredge ("Anson O. Kittredge," 1903, p. 10) was known for his working systems, especially for manufacturing entities (see Romeo and Kyj, 2000, pp. 125–132). And Charles Dutton provided insights into the accounting systems used in the emerging telephone industry (Webster, 1954, p. 13).

Auditing

Auditing, however, had not been an early primary focus in IA circles (cf., the discussion in McMillan, 1998a, p. 121; 1998b, pp. 91, 184–190). Some attention was devoted to explaining the role of accountants in unearthing embezzlements and frauds (see Raymond, 1883; Sprague, 1883). One set of early articles about auditing that appeared in a U.S. journal was taken from a lecture that had been given in England (Slocombe, 1882, 1883). One early editorial in a U.S. journal discussed the role of accountants in auditing in England and suggested the formation of assurance companies in the U.S. that would "guarantee" the accuracy of a firm's accounting records ("Notes and Comments," 1883, pp. 234–235).

But in the 1890s interest in auditing increased because of the above noted formation of great industrial enterprises during the increase in industrial mergers at the end of the nineteenth and the beginning of the twentieth centuries (see the discussion in

Miranti, 1990, p. 49; Allen and McDermott, 1993, pp. 3, 19–21; Lamoreaux, 1985, chapter 1; Wilkins, 1989, pp. 542–543). The curriculum of NYU's SCAF, developed in part by leaders of the IA, contained a course in auditing that addressed "Methods of procedure in examination of accounts of Individuals, Partners, Corporations, Municipalities, etc.: Verification of Balance Sheets and Statements of Profit and Loss; Special Reports" ("New York University School of Commerce, Accounts & Finance," 1901a, p. 16). Also, IA leader A.O. Kittredge briefly wrote on the topic (Kittredge, 1903). In addition, at least one effort was made to increase the awareness of professional accountants about the potentialities of auditing as a technique in promoting more effective corporate governance.[15]

Accounting knowledge and the problem of social ordering

The rise of the IA occurred during an important transitional period in American history that had implications for how pioneering accounting leaders thought accounting knowledge could be applied in achieving a more satisfactory ordering of society (see the discussion in Miranti, 1993a, p. x). The U.S. during the 1880s and 1890s was in a process of transformation brought about by the forces of "nationalization, industrialization, mechanization, [and] urbanization" (Wiebe, 1967, p. 12, chapter 1, and pp. 13–43; also see the general discussion in McMillan, 1998a, p. 126; 1998b, pp. 12, 95–96). In addition, the U.S. was further transformed by new patterns of immigration (Higham, 1955; McMillan, 1998b, p. 12; also see Miranti, 1993, p. x). Although they had long attracted newcomers from rural districts and from "Northern and Western" Europe, the nation's emergent cities experienced a great influx of new people with unfamiliar languages, social practices, and religious traditions from the massive immigration out of "Southern and Eastern Europe" after the middle of the 1880s (Wiebe, 1967, p. 14; also see Higham, 1955, chapter 4; Miranti, 1988, p. 362; 1990, p. 9; 1996, p. 14).

Among the developments resulting from these changes were efforts to find more effective ways of coordinating activities within an increasingly "complex and interdependent society" and also of maintaining cherished traditional values that were thought to have contributed to the nation's greatness and uniqueness (Miranti, 1990, p. 9, also see pp. 10, 43; also see the discussion in Wiebe, 1967). Thus, in accounting, as is discussed below, the thinking of some of the professional leaders about the direction of social change likely was conditioned by a desire to create a synthesis that integrated the verities implicit in traditional norms and virtues and the new power for transforming society that was embedded in their professional knowledge.

One manifestation of these perceptions about the connections between knowledge and social ordering was in public policy formulation, an activity in which the IA only played a minor role prior to its drive to secure public accounting legislation in the 1890s, which is discussed again in a later section of our book. Prior to that time it appears that the only reform that the IA sponsored occurred in 1883.[16]

The IA's program, however, helped to foster a social identity based on knowledge and function that had the potential for surmounting the traditional social divisions that had been primarily rooted in region, religion, political party, and national origin. In the 1880s the promise of scientific accountancy functioned as a social solvent for breaking down barriers that might have otherwise kept IA members apart. For example, the IA programs likely created an intellectual bond that united members who had served on opposing sides during the Civil War – e.g., Charles Sprague and Selden Hopkins were soldiers in the Union Army, and Henry Harney was on the opposite side (see, for example, Miranti, 1988, p. 364; 1990, pp. 44–45; 1996, p. 15; Previts and Merino, 1979, pp. 96, 101; Webster, 1954, p. 108; Flesher *et al.*, 1996, p. 51).

Besides creating new social reference categories, at least one prominent member of the IA also thought that accounting knowledge had a role to play in resolving the seemingly bewildering problems arising in an era in which U.S. society was becoming more mechanized, urbanized, and industrialized. Charles Waldo Haskins, as noted above and discussed later, was drawn to the IA in the late 1890s. Haskins, likely in part because of his earlier mathematical training, was receptive to the notion of scientific accountancy (see the discussion in Jordan, 1923, p. 7). From his perspective (see Haskins, 1900a), accounting was a science whose boundaries of understanding had continually evolved since ancient times.[17] In Haskins' case the belief that accounting could function as a powerful tool in social governance seemed to have been vindicated both on a theoretical and pragmatic level by the example of members of his own extended family.[18]

While the problems of a more mechanized, urbanized, and industrialized society seemed susceptible to its power, scientific accountancy initially did not address in a constructive way the growing cultural and racial diversity within the nation's largest cities (see the discussion in Wiebe, 1967, p. 14; also see the discussion in Hays, 1957, pp. 94–99). In the 1880s the reaction within IA circles to such diversity often took the form of insensitive humor that marginalized the image of those not considered to be in the mainstream. Reports, for example, about IA meetings were in a few instances parodied through the recasting of the minutes in Ebonics and the identity of members in stage-comic names such as "Charles Augustus Pineapple" and "Napoleon Taylor" (see Taylor, 1883a, 1883b; 1884). National accents and presumed character traits were also burlesqued in the correspondence and reports of examining committee interviews of prospective members of foreign background. Again the emphasis was placed on what seemed to be mirthful aspects of unusual accents such as that of an untutored Irishman and of an obsequious German who were candidates for membership (Kelley, 1882; Donderundblitzen, 1883).

Later, however, the insensitive facetiousness about national origins and race ultimately appears to have given way to a more intensive desire to proselytize newcomers to American ways (see the discussion in Miranti, 1988, p. 364; 1990, pp. 43–44). This new attitude was very likely reflected in the outlook of Haskins, who, doubtless, was favorably impressed by the positive opinion that Emerson held about the favorable potentials for foreign immigrants in American society (Gabriel and Walker, 1986, p. 46; Miranti, 1988, p. 364; 1990, p. 51; also see the discussion in Curti, 1964, p. 309). In Haskins' case, however, we sense that the solution to what was considered to be the problem of diversity lay in acculturation. Haskins, who served as an officer for the patriotic society, the Sons of the American Revolution, was a leader of an organization that was attempting to head off potential social conflict and alienation by sponsoring programs to proselytize new arrivals by means of publications and education relating to the established practices of their adopted country (Miranti, 1988, p. 364; 1990, pp. 43–44).

While this attitude represented an improvement over the more callous indifference of the 1880s, it still had shortcomings. First, it appears to have remained silent about the issue of race. This may have been due in part to the fact that at the beginning of the twentieth century in New York City the African–American population was very small in comparison to the total population of the city (see U.S. Census Office, 1902, pp. 138–139).[19] Second, although the Americanization programs were intended to promote integration and comity, new immigrants had the formidable task of rejecting their own traditions and learning to accept norms and values that likely were very different than those of their native countries. Further, notwithstanding any educational programs, the recent immigrant still had to assimilate a new culture and compete with individuals who, along with their families, had long since assimilated and perhaps helped shape the existing culture (see the general discussion in Perlmutter, 1996, pp. 3–4, 30–31, 45, 115–116; Makielski, 1973, chapter 2; Korman, 1965, pp. 396–399; Barrett, 1992, pp. 997–1002; Gerstle, 1997). And both of these problems would continue to plague both the accounting profession and the society it operated in for decades to come. These latter problems, however, were more amenable to politics than science. And they would become central issues in the future politics not only of the nation but also of its microcosm, the professional association (see, e.g., the discussion in Miranti, 1988, pp. 375–376; 1990, chapters 6, 9, 10; also see, e.g., Hammond, 2002).

Nor was an accepting attitude toward foreigners easy for IA members to embrace when it affected their own economic well-being. This was starkly demonstrated by the use of nationalism to enhance the position of IA members in their competition with elite British accountants in the local markets in the U.S. for services starting in the 1890s (see the discussion in Miranti, 1988; 1990, chapters 1–3). The IA's leaders encouraged a strong American national identification to distinguish itself from the competing AAPA, which, because of the latter's "[identification] with British professional traditions" (Miranti, 1990, p. 45), was open to criticism of being foreign and alien. As we shall see in the following Section, these nationalistic impulses played a central role in the later competition to provide order in public accounting in the State of New York accounting through legislation that established the CPA designation.

5 Decline of the IA

The rise of public accounting in the U.S. and the establishment of accountancy laws to regulate these new professional endeavors contributed to the decline of the IA by disrupting the unity of its many specialist groups. Although, as discussed later, the IA played a leading role in promoting public accounting legislation in New York State, its actions ironically helped to crystallize new attitudes among its members about the purposes of professional organizations. The competition with the AAPA over accounting legislation demonstrated the importance of professional and political objectives over considerations of fellowship and mutual assistance that had figured so prominently at the IA's founding. Moreover, it was such an emphasis on professional and political objectives that likely motivated the IA's dynamic public accountants to try to enhance their own professional status by helping launch two highly specialized institutions, in 1897 the New York State Society of Certified Public Accountants (NYSSCPA) (Committee on History, 1953a) and in 1900 NYU's SCAF (Committee on History, 1953b, p. 262). These new institutions, in part, may have been the result of a decision of the leadership of the IA to retain its traditional programs, but to move to a national venue and not to participate in the CPA movement. The programs of these new entities gradually drew members away from the IA and further differentiated public accounting from other parts of accounting practice in terms of status, function, and expertise.

In this section we analyze how these changes, brought about by a desire to establish state-mandated boundaries for public accountancy, eventually fostered the IA's decline.

Role in establishing CPA designation

Although the chronology of the rivalry between the IA and the AAPA in establishing licensing in New York State has been documented elsewhere (e.g., Wilkinson, 1903, pp. 414–416; Carey, 1969, chapter 4; Edwards, 1960, chapters IV and V; Previts and Merino, 1979, pp. 96–98; Miranti, 1988, pp. 366–373; 1990, pp. 48–56; 1996, pp. 14–18; Webster, 1954, see pp. 166–201, 214–236; McMillan, 1998b, pp. 156–159, 200–206), these episodes provide two insights into the nature of professional association functioning in modern American society. The first was the critical role that contacts with governmental bodies played in advancing the goals of professional groups (see the general discussion in Galambos, n.d., pp. 42–47). And the second was how import-ant the maintenance of internal cohesion among the varied elements within a profession was in efforts to deal effectively with government. Cohesion was vital, not only because of the political leverage it gave professional leaders, but also because governmental officials lacked the requisite expertise to judge professional matters and, thus, were only inclined to support policies that had broad support among all shades of opinion within practitioner communities (see the discussion in Miranti, 1988, pp. 374–375; 1996, pp. 16–17; and the general discus-sion in Miranti, 1990, pp. 10–11).

College of Accounts and Professional Accreditation

The bitter fruits of intra-professional conflict soon became apparent in the first episode in which the IA helped to derail the AAPA's drive to establish a College of Accounts for regulating entry into the new profession. This negative outcome demonstrated how critical relationships between leaders of professional bodies and powerful government officials could be in shaping professional governance. In this case the key nexus was the one which unified leaders of the IA and Melvil Dewey, Secretary to the State Board of Regents, the agency responsible for licensing professions and accrediting colleges (Miranti, 1988, pp. 367–368; 1990, pp. 50–52).

The AAPA's plan envisioned the launching of a degree-granting college to train junior accountants as a first step in creating a new system for controlling entrance to the profession (Miranti, 1988, pp. 366–367; 1990, p. 50; Webster, 1954, pp. 166–201). Some AAPA leaders also harbored the hope that the scope of the college's program might eventually include the issuance of a master's degree to certify seasoned experts (Webster, 1954, p. 173; Miranti, 1988, p. 367). Moreover, the development of education in universities was occurring in law, medicine, and engineering (see the discussion in Collins, 1979, pp. 141–142, 150–155, 163–171; Calvert, 1967, chapters 3–5; McMillan, 1998b, pp. 118–119). And more recently in 1881 the University of Pennsylvania had formed its specialized Wharton School to train individuals for careers in business administration (Sass, 1982, chapters 1 and 2). While Webster (1954, p. 164) notes that Wharton's early curriculum did not have a course in "auditing, accounting, or bookkeeping," Pierson and Others (1959, p. 37) indicate that some accounting was taught at Wharton (also see Sass, 1982, p. 46; McMillan, 1998b, p. 129). Also, as noted earlier, Webster (1954, p. 108) notes that Hopkins wrote a book on bookkeeping that had been adopted at Wharton.

The major impediment to the AAPA's plan, however, was that Secretary Dewey decided to exercise his discretion in regard to this proposal in a way that was sensitive to the preferences of his two friends who were members of the IA – Colonel Sprague and Silas Packard. Dewey's connection with Sprague likely derived from their mutual interests in languages and the Modern Language Association (Miranti, 1988, p. 367; 1990, pp. 50, 203 n. 9; 1996, p. 15). As noted earlier, while still on the faculty of Columbia College, Dewey had made use of

Sprague's accounting acumen by inviting the latter to lecture on this topic at the School of Library Economy during 1887 (McMillan, 1998b, p. 44; 1998c, pp. 18–19; also see the general discussion in "Mathematical Elucidation of Accounts," 1887, p. 103). From Sprague's perspective the AAPA's educational initiative was probably worrisome because it threatened to displace the IA as a certifier of expertise and, perhaps, as a deliverer of education. Dewey's connection with Packard, on the other hand, came about through "their mutual interest in vocational education" (Miranti, 1988, p. 367; 1990, p. 50). It was possible that, to Packard, the AAPA's proposed institution was problematic because it sought to carve out a niche in the accounting education market, thus perhaps, competing with his proprietary academy.

Dewey likely assisted the IA by persuading the Regents to limit the scope of the AAPA educational plan (Miranti 1988, pp. 367–368; 1990, pp. 51–52; also see Miranti, 1996, p. 15). Dewey likely consulted with Sprague who attended the AAPA's petitioning meeting (The Committee on History, 1952, p. 432; Webster, 1954, p. 175). The Regents determined that its proposed college's 1,000 hour curriculum did not justify it becoming a degree-giving institution (Miranti, 1988, pp. 366–368; 1990, p. 52; 1996, p. 15; Miranti and Goodman, 1996, p. 36). The Regents allowed the AAPA provisionally to form a school (Webster, 1954, p. 190). The school, which opened during October 1893, survived for one academic year (Miranti, 1988, p. 369; 1990, p. 52; Webster, 1954, pp. 196–199). Factors such as the downgrading of its program and limited registrations due to a severe business downturn induced the AAPA to abandon its educational initiative in 1894 (Webster, 1954, pp. 197–198; Miranti, 1988, p. 369; 1990, p. 52; 1996, p. 15).

Lobbying for public accounting legislation

A similar pattern illustrating the importance of the nexus between practitioner groups and government and the importance of cohesion within and between such groups was also apparent in the second episode, the competition to secure public accounting legislation. The initiative again was taken by the AAPA responding to a suggestion put forward by Secretary Dewey in March 1894 that accounting should be professionalized through legislation (see Webster, 1954, p. 217). By February 1895 the AAPA sponsored a bill written by practitioner Francis Gottsberger and introduced into the Legislature by State Senator Daniel Bradley (Wilkinson, 1903, pp. 414–415; Committee on History, 1953a, p. 220). Part of the proposed legislation seemed designed to revive the notion of a qualifying school of accounts as part of a gateway for new individuals to enter the profession (Webster, 1954, pp. 222–223).

By focusing on the Legislature rather than the Regents, the AAPA apparently hoped to counter the IA's advantageous relationship with Dewey. In another move that placed Dewey in a potentially embarrassing conflict with his IA allies, members of the AAPA protested to the Regents about the IA's issuing "'certified accountant's degrees'" (Miranti, 1988, p. 369; also see Miranti, 1990, p. 46; 1996, p. 14; Miranti and Goodman, 1996, p. 35). The IA parried the AAPA's legislative thrust by introducing its own bill whose authorship Webster (1954, pp. 215–217) attributes to mainly Colonel Sprague, and Wilkinson (1903, p. 414; 1928, p. 264) attributes to Henry Harney.[20] In early March of 1895, ". . . the [IA's] bill was introduced in the Assembly by . . . Howard Payton Wilds, Assemblyman for one of the Manhattan Island districts . . ." (Wilkinson, 1903, p. 415). The essence of the bill was the creation of an examining process for a new class of experts known as a "'certified public accountant'" (Miranti, 1988, p. 369; 1990, p. 53; also see Miranti, 1996, p. 16). The bill also required the examination applicant to be a citizen of the U.S. (Miranti, 1988, pp. 369–370; 1990, p. 53; 1996, p. 16). This requirement would have been detrimental to British AAPA members who were not U.S. citizens (Miranti, 1988, p. 370; 1990, p. 53; 1996, p. 16).

Although neither the IA nor the AAPA succeeded in 1895, with some measure of cooperation between the groups a licensing law was secured during the following year.[21] The resultant CPA law enacted on 17 April 1896 conformed closely to the IA draft (Webster, 1954, p. 234; also see, e.g., Wilkinson, 1903, p. 416). The law, however, allowed both a U.S. citizen and an individual who had the intent of becoming a U.S. citizen to become certified (Miranti, 1988, p. 372; 1990, p. 56; 1996, p. 18; Flesher *et al.*, 1996, p. 51). Also, the 1896 law (see "Institute of Accounts," 1896, p. 259) did not include a provision in the original IA bill that would have restricted work "'as examiners of accounts, expert accountants or paid auditors'" performed for certain governmental bodies and officials to CPAs (Wilkinson, 1903, p. 415).

Organizational developments

The establishment of the CPA designation set into motion organizational developments that eventually had negative consequences for the IA's long-term viability. Emergent professional entities differentiated themselves from the IA by embracing either or both of two broad objectives. The first was the advancement of the specific interests of the rising class of CPAs. The second was the transmittal of CPA legislation beyond the boundaries of New York State. Thus, the emerging professional associations were attempting to become catalysts for and leaders of progressive change.

Although the IA had been a primary vehicle for promoting public accounting legislation, its leaders abandoned any desire to become identified with particular functional outlets for accountancy (such as public accounting), preferring to dedicate their organization's energies exclusively to the promotion of what they believed was their special science within the spheres of business and economics. As IA President Charles Dutton expressed it in 1897:

> The Institute of Accounts is unique as an exponent of the element of accounting and the science of accounts, for it

stands between business and its promoters and transactors, as an interpreter of the elements and principles of economics. Its functions briefly stated are these: To secure a proper recognition of Accounting as an element of business. To discover new principles of accounting, and to orderly arrange them for the enlargement of the science. To originate and to circulate the literature of Accountics. To maintain the dignity and uphold the importance of the profession of accountancy. To broaden the scope of the science of political economy. To establish a harmonious relation of mutual dependence between itself and the business world, and to induce able and experienced men everywhere to devote their energies, in association with it, to the accomplishment of its purposes.

(Dutton, 1897, p. 5)

The IA's primary organizational initiative, which began in 1897, involved its restructuring as a generalist national body operating through local chapters (Webster, 1954, p. 282; "Nationalization of the Institute of Accounts," 1897, p. 14). Although, as noted earlier, IA chapters were launched in at least Massachusetts, New York City, Washington, D.C., Hartford (Connecticut), and perhaps Chicago, only the New York City chapter (which was the original IA) survived past 1901 ("New York Accountants' Headquarters," 1897, p. 82; "Massachusetts Institute of Accounts," 1897, p. 67; "Washington Chapter of the Institute of Accounts," 1898, p. 93; "Hartford Chapter," 1898a, p. 124; "Hartford Chapter," 1898b, pp. 3–6; Webster, 1954, pp. 280–284; "The Institute of Accounts," 1897; "Official Roster of Accountants' Associations," 1897a, 1897b). Thus, the leadership of the IA abdicated the historic role the IA had played as the catalyst of and leader of progressive professional change. Instead, the IA leadership attempted to maintain the status quo, but on a national basis. This was a crucial decision that likely was a key factor in the IA becoming a transitional organization.

The IA's unwillingness to make the CPA movement a

primary associational concern undoubtedly influenced some IA members to become affiliated with two emergent CPA associations based in New York City. As noted earlier (see note 6 and Figure 1.1), the National Society of Certified Public Accountants (NSCPA) was established in 1897. The NSCPA, as its name implied, sought to promote the CPA movement nationally (Miranti, 1990, p. 59). Although it appears that a small number of NSCPA members such as Joseph Hardcastle were drawn from the IA, a number of NSCPA members were drawn from the AAPA and one or more NSCPA members may have been members of both the IA and the AAPA (see "National Society of Certified Public Accountants," 1897, p. 110; also see "The National Society of Certified Public Accountants in the United States," 1899, p. 39; "The American Association of Public Accountants," 1899, pp. 40–41). In addition to promoting CPA legislation, the NSCPA also likely attracted members by promising to establish a professional library similar to one established "by the Institute of Chartered Accountants of Great Britain" ("National Society of Certified Public Accountants," 1897, p. 110). Although one source indicated that in early 1899 the NSCPA had 83 members ("The National Society of Certified Public Accountants in the United States," 1899, p. 39), its impact on professional affairs was short lived and minor. The NSCPA's influence waned even before the establishment of the Federation of State Societies of Public Accountants in the United States of America (Federation) in 1902, which also sought to promote the CPA profession (see the discussion in Miranti, 1990, pp. 49, 59).[22] After decades of dormancy, the NSCPA finally was merged into the AIA in 1941 (Webster, 1954, p. 290).[23]

Much more significant was the organizational "meeting of the" NYSSCPA on the 30th of March in 1897 ("New York State Society of Certified Public Accountants," 1897, pp. 14–15), an event that closely coincided with the reorganization of the IA as a national entity (see the discussion in "Nationalization of the Institute of Accounts," 1897, p. 14; The Committee on History, 1949, p. 327; Horne, 1947, p. 5).

All but one of the individuals who were signatories to the document incorporating the NYSSCPA belonged to the IA (see Committee on History, 1953a, pp. 217–222; Kyj and Romeo, 1997, p. 11). Moreover, unlike the NSCPA, the NYSSCPA had by its very nature the responsibility for protecting the interests of CPAs within the State of New York, although as we shall see below the NYSSCPA eventually was drawn into the promotion of the CPA credential throughout the U.S. through its membership in the Federation.

The transition of some IA members to the rising NYSSCPA likely was facilitated by the personal influence of a new professional leader, Charles Waldo Haskins, who as noted earlier and discussed below was one of the individuals who established the firm of Haskins & Sells. As we shall see in the following Section, Haskins' career exemplified what could be achieved in public accountancy. Consequently, it is likely that some practitioners in the IA transferred their primary associational allegiance to the NYSSCPA, an organization Haskins presided over from its founding until his death in 1903 (see, e.g., NYSSCPA, 1927, p. 5).

The background of a paragon of professional virtue

In addition to his personal skills and energy, Haskins' meteoric rise in the new CPA profession was partly propelled by his ties to New York's social elite.[24] During 1893 Haskins received a prestigious appointment to assist "a joint commission of congress" ("Haskins, Charles Waldo," 1907, p. 515) which was briefly discussed earlier in our book. During this assignment he worked with (see, e.g., "Haskins, Charles Waldo," 1907, p. 515) and eventually "formed a copartnership with Elijah [Watt] Sells" ("Haskins, Charles Waldo," 1907, p. 515; also see Haskins & Sells, 1970, pp. 10, 12, 13; Jordan, 1923, p. 53). More specifically, on the 4th of March of 1895, the commission went out of existence and Haskins & Sells began its operations in a Manhattan location (Jordan, 1923, p. 53; Haskins & Sells, 1970, pp. 12, 13).

Haskins and the IA

Early in his career Haskins may have had contact with the IA. Haskins possibly corresponded with the *American Counting-room* in 1884 to provide his views on and to ask for the thoughts of others on how to record certain real estate transactions ("Real Estate Accounts," 1884, pp. 165–166). As discussed later, Haskins does not appear to have joined the IA until 1899 ("New York Chapter of the Institute of Accounts," 1899, p. 138).

In 1889, Haskins resigned from the AAPA but rejoined in 1901 (Webster, 1954, p. 352), while Colonel Sprague apparently was never a member (see Webster, 1954). Although no known record explains these choices, the later activities of both men suggest, perhaps, that their decisions were probably partially affected by their advocacy of accounting science (cf., McMillan, 1998b, pp. 150, 153). This latter belief was not shared by a number in the AAPA who, instead, viewed accounting as an art involving loose approximations of economic realities and whose practice was highly dependent on the subjective views of an experienced expert (Miranti, 1988, pp. 365–366; 1990, p. 39).

Haskins's and Sprague's ties to patriotic associations also suggest that they probably looked askance at a professional body like the AAPA that identified with a "foreign" model of professionalism (see Miranti, 1988, p. 364; 1990, pp. 43–45; "Charles E. Sprague, Ph.D.," 1897, p. 129). To many strong nationalists of this era, imperial Britain likely was viewed as a nemesis to American diplomacy (see the discussion in Campbell, 1976, chapter 11).[25] And yet another possible unifying factor was the likely belief shared by many native accountants that the market was saturated with too many accountants and that the AAPA was aggravating this problem by helping to promote the interests and ideals of the chartered accountants (see the general discussion in Miranti, 1988, pp. 362, 364; 1990, pp. 44–46).

The sudden prominence of Haskins on the professional scene

ultimately had an important bearing on the decisions taken in 1896 by Secretary Dewey in determining the composition of the members of the board that would examine individuals wishing to become CPAs – "the Board of Examiners" ("Institute of Accounts," 1896, p. 259). It is possible that the initial conception may have been that the board's membership should be reflective of three groups: the AAPA, the IA, and independents unaffiliated with any professional body. After consultation with Sprague and Packard, Dewey decided to appoint Sprague, who appears to have been the IA's representative, and Frank Broaker, who appears to have been chosen to represent the AAPA (see Miranti, 1988, pp. 372–373; 1990, p. 56; 1996, p. 18; "Institute of Accounts," 1896, p. 259). Continuing this line of reasoning, the question of an independent candidate was, likely, more difficult to resolve because of the lack of any clear-cut, organizational support. It was, nevertheless, important because such an appointee's vote would resolve any disputes that arose between representatives of the rival bodies. This vote proved to be especially critical in judging whether particular candidates qualified to receive a certificate under the waiver provision (see the discussion in Miranti, 1988, pp. 372–373; 1990, pp. 57–58). Waiver served as a major portal of entry into the CPA profession in the State of New York, especially during its formative years (see Edwards, 1960, pp. 352–353).

Dewey's eventual choice of Haskins to fill the third slot on the Board of Examiners likely was predicated on the assessment of a complex set of factors. The first was the likely positive effect that Haskins' appointment would have on Dewey's relationship to some members of the New York Board of Regents. Haskins knew, for example, Regents Chauncey Depew (a state senator) and William Croswell Doane (Miranti, 1988, p. 367; 1990, p. 51). Haskins, Depew, and Doane were all active in the Sons of the American Revolution (Miranti, 1988, p. 367; 1990, p. 51). In addition, Haskins' ties to the Havemeyers was likely important to Dewey (see, e.g., the general discussion in Miranti, 1988, p. 367; 1990, p. 51). There likely were other reasons that also persuaded Dewey. For example, Elijah Watt Sells recommended Haskins to him and then saw to it that a request was made to a number of individuals with influence to send recommendations in favor of Haskins' appointment on the eve of the Regent's decision about the composition of the Board of Examiners (Jordan, 1923, pp. 59–61). Haskins received the appointment (see, e.g., "Haskins, Charles Waldo," 1907, p. 515; Jordan, 1923, p. 61).

After the passage of CPA legislation in New York, Haskins began to draw closer to the IA whose national president in 1897 was Charles Sprague, his colleague from the Board of Examiners ("Institute of Accounts (National)," 1897, p. 100; also see Kittredge, 1897, p. 68). This bridge building was probably a natural consequence of the previously noted fact that some of the founders of the NYSSCPA, in which Haskins served as its first president (see, e.g., NYSSCPA, 1927, p. 5), were also IA members. Haskins appears to have become an icon to the practitioners within this latter organization symbolizing how their long-held beliefs in the promise of accounting science could be translated into a strong record of accomplishment in the rising CPA profession.

Haskins appears to have begun to interact with the IA starting in 1897 (Kittredge, 1897, p. 68) and to have become a member in 1899 ("New York Chapter of the Institute of Accounts," 1899, p. 138). In 1900, he presented a lengthy lecture on the evolution of accounting ("New York Chapter of the Institute of Accounts," 1900, p. 25) that was subsequently published in *Accountics* (Haskins, 1900a, pp. 33–34, 51, 69–70). Further, Haskins gave other accountants hope and was living proof of the potential of careers in public accountancy. IA members could identify closely on a personal level with his career. Haskins' experience demonstrated how an individual, who shared much the same gentrified backgrounds as some IA members (see, e.g., "Haskins, Charles Waldo," 1907, pp. 514–515), could use the insights provided by accounting science to achieve great personal success in providing services to some of the most important business and governmental entities that were reshaping American civilization. Also, those IA members who joined the NYSSCPA thus became part of an association (the NYSSCPA) that was actively promoting progressive professional change.

But Haskins, of course, was much more than a mere symbol of change. He was a real action hero who played a central role in launching two new organizations – the NYSSCPA and NYU's SCAF – which helped to transform accounting and, by so doing, set into motion new circumstances leading to the eventual demise of the IA as a professional force (see the discussion in Miranti, 1996, p. 18). The first step in this progression had been the previously mentioned founding in 1897 of the NYSSCPA, an organization dedicated to the promotion of the interests of those who had earned the new professional credential (see Horne, 1947, p. 6; The Committee on History, 1949, 1953a; Miranti, 1993a, p. ix).

The NYSSCPA thrived because of this dedication to the interests of members of a growing CPA community. The new entity became even more strongly committed to the preservation of the structure of professionalism brought into being by the 1896 legislation than the IA. Although some IA members became certified, those who did not receive licenses such as Edward C. Cockey (Board of Examiners of Public Accountants, 1897, pp. 29–31; Webster, 1954, pp. 255–256), the IA's founding president, likely, did not favor having the resources of their organization used to promote policies beneficial to CPAs. Moreover, as we have mentioned already, the IA became more closely identified with the broad promotion of accounting knowledge rather than its narrow application for any particular specialized function (Dutton, 1897, pp. 5–6; Loeb, 2000c, p. 19). It is this combination of the IA's promotion of accounting knowledge, its lack of concern with the market opportunity that was associated with the rise of public accounting, and its loss of status as a leader of progressive professional change, that likely was key to the IA's decline (cf., Romeo and Kyj, 1998, pp. 42–45).

Many New York CPAs likely favored the NYSSCPA because of its concern for the interests of CPAs. Such interest was illustrated by the opposition the NYSSCPA mounted to the incorporation of the Accounting Guarantee Company ("Accounting Guarantee Company," 1897, p. 44). This proposed entity was to be formed "to do a general expert accounting business" but the NYSSCPA was concerned that this would be done "without the condition of taking out a certificate under the State law" ("Accounting Guarantee Company," 1897, p. 44).

Further, new entrants to the CPA profession were more likely to be drawn to the NYSSCPA or the AAPA, which were dedicated to public accountancy and progressive professional change, rather than the functionally amorphous and more conservative IA (see the discussion in McMillan, 1998b, pp. 85–86; 1999, pp. 25–26). From the perspective of new entrants to the CPA profession, membership in an organization like the IA, which had long admitted bookkeepers, likely seemed inappropriate, especially in light of the potential negative comments that such an affiliation might engender from colleagues who were members only of public accounting oriented associations.

School of Commerce, Accounts and Finance (SCAF)

The *second* organizational innovation in which Haskins and the NYSSCPA played a key role was in the formation of NYU's SCAF, a development that eventually co-opted the IA's traditional function as an educational institution and the dispenser of the truths of scientific accountancy. A special NYSSCPA committee consisting of Leon Brummer, Henry R.M. Cook (chair), Charles W. Haskins, Anson O. Kittredge, and John R. Loomis was appointed to look into the development of an accounting school (Committee on History, 1953b, p. 261). NYU eventually agreed to establish such a school (see, e.g., Jordan, 1923, p. 66). Haskins is credited with playing a key role in the process of convincing NYU to establish the school and may even have offered to be a guarantor of the fiscal viability of such a school (see the discussion in Jordan, 1923, pp. 63–66; Society Release, 1959, p. 359; Miranti, 1988, p. 365; 1990, p. 42; 1993a, p. xi).

NYU's SCAF opened in October 1900 with Charles Waldo Haskins as its dean and a faculty that initially drew heavily from the ranks of the IA (see Haskins, 1900b, p. 411; "The Members of the Faculty of New York University School of Commerce, Accounts, and Finance," 1900, pp. 412–413; Committee on History, 1953b, p. 262; Miranti, 1996, p. 18; McMillan, 1998b, pp. 233–235). Haskins (1900b, p. 409) in an article published in the September 1900 issue of *Business: The Office Paper and the Public Accountant* suggests that the establishment of SCAF was, in part, an effort to address the educational needs that were a consequence of New York's CPA law. Also, the "Object of the School" noted in apparent advertisements relating to NYU's SCAF published in *Commerce, Accountants & Finance* suggests a close relationship between the initial curriculum of SCAF and the New York State CPA credential (see, e.g., "New York University School of Commerce, Accounts & Finance," 1901a, p. 16).

The change in organizational commitment among the chief proponents of scientific accounting was also evinced in 1900 by the replacement of *Accountics*, which had closely tracked the affairs of the IA since 1897 and, as noted earlier, had been the IA's official publication, with *Commerce, Accounts & Finance*. This latter publication focused more closely on the activities of the accountants who were associated with the NYSSCPA and NYU's SCAF (see the general discussion in McMillan, 1998b, p. 236).

Effect of the failed nationalization of the IA

Paralleling these changes was an abortive drive of the IA to maintain its leadership in professional affairs in light of the growing competition from the NYSSCPA and the AAPA. Central to the IA's strategy for survival was its reorganization as a national entity, a move that was likely aimed at maintaining existing programs at a national level and at attracting cost and managerial accountants, bankers, credit managers, and other members of the business community rather than public accountants. Such efforts were exemplified by the election in 1897 of a banker to the IA's national presidency and also by Kittredge's connections with banking and other providers of credit.[26] This state of affairs became obvious by 1902 when the IA was not included in a new umbrella organization, the Federation, formed to coordinate public accounting legislation nationwide (Miranti, 1990, p. 49). Instead, the NYSSCPA along with various emergent state public accountancy associations helped form the Federation as a national association (Miranti, 1990, pp. 62–63).[27] In 1905 the Federation merged with the AAPA (Webster, 1954, p. 317).[28] While annual national conventions were held by the IA from 1897 to 1901, it was significant that apparently only New York members attended the last such conclave (Webster, 1954, p. 284).

Romeo and Kyj (1998, p. 42) report finding a published meeting notice relating to the IA as late as early 1907. The May 1908 issue of *The Journal of Accountancy* includes an article by George Wilkinson that was from a speech he gave in late April of 1908 and that article, in part, discusses the IA (see Wilkinson, 1908, especially pp. 45, 48–50; also see Romeo and Kyj, 1998, p. 44 n. 17). Wilkinson (1908, pp. 48–49) suggests that at the time the IA was having monthly meetings and that the IA's key function was education. He (1908, p. 49) suggests that the IA apparently was a functioning organization of around 135 members. Wilkinson (1908, p. 49) suggests that the IA was still requiring prospective members to satisfy IA examiners, but no longer granted C.A. certification. Additionally, he (1908, p. 49) suggests that the IA had members located not only in New York City, but also in other areas in the U.S.

Wilkinson (1908, p. 50) indicates that in 1908, Henry Harney was the President of the IA. Another source (Committee on History, 1953a, p. 221) indicates that until he passed away in May of 1910, Henry Harney was active in the IA. However, until 1940 these are the last references to some type of current activity relating to the IA that we have located. Thus, it is likely that the IA became dormant during the second decade of the twentieth century. Although, as noted earlier, the IA survived until 1940 (see Figure 1.1), it was, as suggested earlier, the combination of the IA's promotion of accounting knowledge, its lack of concern with the market opportunity that was associated with the rise of public accounting, and its loss of status as a leader of progressive professional change that destined the IA to pass the following years as a shell.

6 Legacy

The question remains: what legacy did the IA leave for posterity? Until recently, accounting historians for several reasons have largely overlooked the significance of the IA. First, its associational records have long been lost (Webster, 1954, p. 12). Second, a number of the articles of its leading thinkers, such as Hardcastle, Sprague, and Kittredge, were not included in the inaugural edition of the *Accountants' Index* (1921). In fact, this latter problem was not really overcome until Garland Publishing, Inc. reprinted the journals (cf., Loeb, 2002b, p. 9) that had conveyed the ideas of IA luminaries (e.g., Sprague, 1880b, 1901; Hardcastle, 1883a, 1883b, 1884; Kittredge, 1880, 1897, 1900). And lastly some standard references on professional history such as the works of Webster (1954), Edwards (1960), and Carey (1969), which emphasized the AAPA, tended to treat the IA as a transitional entity and did not seek to evaluate what lasting impact it may have had on professional accounting (see McMillan, 1998b, pp. 7–8, 137).

As we have seen, however, the IA was a pioneer in the development of many of the activities and characteristics that we today associate with accounting professionalism (see Romeo and Kyj, 1998, pp. 45–47). For example, as noted earlier, the IA had lobbied government as early as the 1880s to seek revisions of state banking law. The IA also began the process of admission based on examination and of formally denoting different categories of membership based on successful completion of qualifying examinations (see Romeo and Kyj, 1998, pp. 36–37, 40–41, 45, 46; McMillan, 1998b, pp. 67–69, 74–75; 1999, pp. 15–16, 19–20). Also, the IA took the lead in enhancing professional knowledge through its sponsorship of lectures and discussions that were roughly akin to continuing professional education in the contemporary profession, the formation of a library, and its support of professional periodicals. Moreover, the IA was an early agent in the process of fostering a professional consciousness and of advancing the interests of accountants on a national level (cf., Romeo and Kyj, 1998, pp. 45–47).

Besides these general professional attributes, leaders of the IA were pioneers in defining accounting's cognitive base and the ways that this knowledge should be conveyed through formal educational processes. Consider, for example, their influence on accounting education. While we agree with McMillan (1998b, pp. 53–54; 1998c, pp. 28–29) that the IA's notions of scientific accounting had a strong influence in the academy, we believe these impacts initially had the greatest effect on pedagogy. Only later did these notions begin to exert much influence over theory building. Although the programs of the Wharton School antedated those of NYU's SCAF by more than a decade, the emphasis on accounting science and professionalism at the latter school was much more akin to modern academic schools, departments, or programs of accountancy (see the general discussion in Roy and MacNeill, 1966; McMillan, 1998b, pp. 53–54; 1998c, pp. 28–29; "New York University School of Commerce, Accounts & Finance," 1901a, p. 16; "New York University School of Commerce, Accounts and Finance," 1901b, p. 1).

The program that Haskins headed was following the lead of engineering, a profession he had prepared for at "Polytechnic Institute of Brooklyn" (Jordan, 1923, p. 7) and which had begun a shift from apprenticeships to collegiate programs as the primary mode of training during the century that just ended (see the discussion in Calvert, 1967, chapters 3–5; Collins, 1979, pp. 163–171). This approach also had an appeal because it corresponded to the trends apparent in legal and medical education (see the discussion in Collins, 1979, pp. 141–142, 150–155; McMillan, 1998b, pp. 118–119). The curriculum of the new professional school incorporated the idea of the inter-connectedness between accounting and other forms of specialized business knowledge (see "New York University School of Commerce, Accounts & Finance," 1901a, p. 16; "New York University School of Commerce, Accounts and Finance," 1901b, p. 1). New accountants were not only to be specialists in their own field but were to have a strong grasp of the general principles controlling understanding of the broader context of commerce and finance (see "New York University School of Commerce, Accounts & Finance," 1901a, p. 16; "New York University School of Commerce, Accounts and Finance," 1901b, p. 1).

Attempts to develop a more comprehensive theoretical framework for accounting progressed slowly due in part perhaps to the death of key proponents of accounting science. By the end of 1906, Haskins (1903), Kittredge (1903), and Hardcastle (1906) had all died, and Sprague passed from the scene in 1912, albeit not before he had published *The Philosophy of Accounts* (1907) (see The Committee on History, 1951, p. 617; Mann, 1931, pp. 58, 66; Society Release, 1959, p. 360; "Anson O. Kittredge," 1903, p. 9; Miranti, 1990, p. 73).

After Haskins, leadership in the new school passed to Dr. Joseph French Johnson, formerly of the Wharton School who, like many in the mainstream in business education, was influenced by the business and professional leaders who hired their graduates and encouraged the prevailing tendency for accounting to be treated as a pragmatic form of knowledge (Miranti 1990, pp. 40–43; also see Sass, 1982, pp. 141–142, 182). Langenderfer (1987, p. 308) notes that "up to the late 1920s [in] accounting education [there was no] research tradition [and] few full-time academics with their Ph.D. degrees. . . ." It was not until 1938 that the initial program specifically leading to a Ph.D. in accounting was begun (Bedford, 1997, p. 21).

The development of theory eventually flourished. Sprague's theoretical contribution had been developed largely from a proprietary perspective suitable for the simple businesses of the nineteenth century and earlier (see, for example, Chatfield, 1974, pp. 220–223; 1996b, p. 481; Previts and Merino, 1979, pp. 165, 168–169). Professor William A. Paton of the University of Michigan, on the other hand, sought to extend the work of both Sprague and Henry Rand Hatfield by developing new theoretical constructs relevant to the modern business corporation, an entity of great scale and scope, whose reporting had to be responsive to the needs of a more complex set of stakeholder relationships (Chatfield, 1996a, pp. 230–231; see Paton, 1962, especially p. xviii; Paton and Littleton, 1940; Thompson, 1996, pp. 453–454).

The IA's notion that accounting was a precise mathematical science did not become a central issue in research and education until the 1960s (Miranti, 1993b, pp. 115–117; see the general discussion in Whitely, 1986; Baskin and Miranti, 1997, pp. 9–11). This change was partly made possible by advances in computational efficiency made possible by computers. Soon scholars began implementing research programs that sought to amplify the accounting effects of the new paradigms derived by financial economists through the application of logical and mathematical processes (see Miranti, 1993b, pp. 115–117 and see the general discussion in Whitely, 1986).

The quantification implicit in scientific accountancy also affected the practice of some public accounting firms. For example, some firms have used statistical sampling in auditing (see, e.g., the discussion in Tucker and Lordi, 1997). Also, the use of analytical techniques to assist in the audits of financial statements is another example of the use of quantitative techniques.

The attempt of the IA to use accounting legislation as a means for restraining market competition by excluding chartered accountants from U.S. professional markets failed. During this early era a CPA certificate did not include restrictions on licensing and thus was, in effect, a badge of professional competency and did not limit access to practice (see, e.g., Edwards, 1960, p. 110; Loeb, 2002d, pp. 46–47). Nor did the 1896 New York accountancy law initially exert any significant influence on a professional service that essentially served the needs of an international capital market. The chartered accounting firms that began opening U.S. branches in the latter part of the nineteenth century were largely intended to verify information about American businesses for foreign stakeholders. These consumers doubtless preferred to rely on the expertise of professional names well known and respected in London which then was the world's largest financial market (e.g., Allen and McDermott, 1993, p. 3; Miranti, 1988, p. 362; 1990, pp. 33–34; Wilkins, 1989, pp. 536–545; Edwards, 1960, p. 50; McMillan, 1998b, pp. 146–150). Eventually, chartered accountants began to provide leadership in promoting public accounting legislation in some U.S. jurisdictions (Miranti, 1988, p. 376; 1990, pp. 61–62; 1996, pp. 18, 20). And their political influence in associational affairs, consequently, was strongly felt when practitioners sought to define institutional arrangements for ordering professional affairs (see the discussion in Miranti, 1988, p. 37; 1990, pp. 73–75).

The use of accounting legislation as a mechanism for restraining market entry would probably have had a deleterious effect on the development of U.S. public accounting. British practitioners enriched American accounting by transferring the product of a lengthy process of professional institutional evolution whose origin dated back to the 1840s (see, e.g., the discussion in Howitt, 1966, chapters 1–3; also in Jones, 1981, chapters 1–4). Without this infusion of foreign talent, the efficiency and effectiveness of the new public accounting profession in serving the information requirements of U.S. capital markets would have been much diminished.

The failure of the IA as a viable representative organization resulted from the inability of its leaders to translate their conceptions about the nature of accounting to a program that could satisfy the professional and market wants of a diverse membership. And in doing so the IA ceased to be an agent of professional progress and progressive professional change (cf., Romeo and Kyj, 1998, pp. 42–45; McMillan, 1999, pp. 25–26). The basic quandary stemmed from the differing roles and perspectives that separated public accountants who functioned as independent contractors from bookkeepers and industrial accountants who were corporate functionaries. Moreover, ideas about the science of accounts, which could have conceivably continued to provide an intellectual common denominator for maintaining unity, became much less important to public accounting members who sought to stress the uniqueness of their expertise to win acceptance for their services in a rapidly expanding industrial capital market. Ultimately, it was the pressures of the market place that compelled public accountants to differentiate their roles more sharply from the more general population of bookkeepers and accountants. And it was the latter imperative that shifted the trend in professional accounting associations decisively toward more narrowly focused professional bodies.

As a transitional organization the IA played the equivalent role in the professionalization of accounting that the ASSA played in the professionalization of social science (see McMillan, 1998b, p. 85; 1999, p. 26; see the discussion in Galambos, 1983, p. 487). In discussing Haskell's (1977) study of the ASSA, Galambos (1983, p. 487) indicates that the ASSA was both "transitional" and "semiprofessional." Galambos (1983, p. 487) notes that

> the ASSA, [Haskell] found, provided scholars with a new mode of inquiry at a time [1865–1909] when the traditional forms of explanation were losing respect. Having made its contribution, the ASSA gave way to more specialized groups. . . .

Drawing on the work of Wiebe (1967, 1975), Galambos (1983, pp. 486–487) suggests that the cohesive nature of specialized associations helped "order" a changing society in the late nineteenth and early twentieth centuries. This need for cohesiveness and order also helps explain why the generalist and semiprofessional IA, as noted earlier, probably became dormant in the second decade of the twentieth century and like the ASSA became a transitional organization.

Haskell (1977, p. vii) notes that

> the ASSA died because its explanation of human affairs began to appear less credible than those of its new professional competitors. The Association's diminished credibility reflects [a] stubborn adherence to a strategy of explanation which ... no longer seemed plausible to serious thinkers of a younger generation. ...

The parallel to the IA with its devotion to the science of accounts and to an organizational strategy developed in the early 1880s is striking.

As noted earlier, the IA did reemerge briefly again in 1940 when it merged with the AIA – now the American Institute of Certified Public Accountants. The merger happened at approximately the same time that the AIA consolidated with the NSCPA, another dormant organization that we discussed earlier in our book.[29] The merger of the IA with the AIA and the consolidation of the NSCPA into the AIA were significant because these acts represented the culmination of a process of professional reunification begun with the election of Robert H. Montgomery of Lybrand, Ross Brothers & Montgomery as president of the AIA in 1935 (Miranti, 1990, p. 168). Since 1921, U.S. public accountancy had been sharply divided into two national factions represented by the AIA and the ASCPA (Miranti, 1990, pp. 120–124).[30] In general, the AIA and ASCPA were distinguished primarily by differences in the nature of practice and social backgrounds of their respective memberships (Miranti, 1990, pp. 120, 123–124).

Inter-associational competition, however, had created public confusion as to the proper source of authority in public accountancy. This problem became acute after the passage of the New

Deal's securities market legislation and the formation of the U.S. Securities and Exchange Commission, an agency whose powers threatened to encroach on the professional prerogatives of a divided practitioner community (see, for example, the discussion in Miranti, 1986b, pp. 460–468). The mergers of the ASCPA, the NSCPA, and the IA with the AIA were crucial steps in restoring harmony because it combined into one surviving organization all of the key national entities that had played prominent roles in promoting professionalism at various junctures during the U.S. public accounting profession's formative years (see the general discussion in Miranti, 1990, pp. 173–177). As the AIA's *1940 Yearbook* noted, the objective of the IA and NSCPA merger/consolidation was to ensure that the AIA was the "successor" to the key "older" associations ("Older Accounting Societies," 1941, p. 125).[31]

The recognition of how vital unity was in preserving professional autonomy persuaded professional leaders to confine their debates over the institutional framework for governing public accounting to a single forum. A revitalized and united AIA became a highly effective instrument for building broad consensus among the profession's varied elements. This, in turn, enabled public accountants to present a single perspective on public policy matters, which gave them political leverage to deflect any unwanted encroachments by other groups (see Miranti, 1986a, p. 108). And the new professional configuration that the AIA promoted was still being influenced by notions about the nature of accounting and its role in society first put forth by Colonel Sprague and his colleagues in their *soirees* during the 1880s and 1890s (cf., Romeo and Kyj, 1998, pp. 46–47).

Notes

1 There is a more detailed discussion of this issue, as it relates to accounting, later in the book.
2 There is a more detailed discussion of this issue, as it relates to accounting, later in the book.
3 Also see Miranti (1993b, pp. 118–119) for a discussion of some of these points.
4 Also see Lipartito and Miranti (1998, pp. 302–303) and Miranti (1993b, p. 120) for a discussion of some of these points.
5 See note 6 for a discussion of the associations noted in Figure 1.1. Also, as discussed later in our book, the IA at its founding was called the Institute of Accountants and Book-keepers of the City of New York ("Institute of Accountants and Book-keepers of the City of New York.," 1882, p. 248). In July of 1886, the group renamed itself Institute of Accounts (IA) ("Change of Name.," 1886, p. 30). In this book, for the most part, we use the name Institute of Accounts (IA) when referring to the association.
6 The current American Institute of Certified Public Accountants (AICPA) has its origins in a number of early associations. Figure 1.1 indicates when each of these early associations was founded, changed names (if this occurred), and became part of what is today the AICPA. The IA is discussed extensively throughout this book. The remainder of the other early associations depicted in Figure 1.1 are briefly described in the remainder of this note and are discussed at various other points in this book. More extensive discussions of these early associations can be found elsewhere (depending on the association, see for example, Webster, 1954; Edwards, 1960; Previts and Merino, 1979; Miranti, 1990).

AAPA

Webster (1954, pp. 24 – 25) traces the beginnings of the AICPA to a meeting in New York City on 22 December 1886. At that meeting Webster (1954, p. 25) notes that records indicate that it was decided to name the organization the "'American Association of Public Accountants'" (AAPA). The next "general" meeting was held on 17 January 1887, certain officers were elected and a "draft constitution" was passed (Webster, 1954, p. 25). The "Certificate of Incorporation . . . was executed on August 20, 1887, and filed on September 20, 1887" (Webster, 1954, p. 26).

NSCPA

Webster (1954, p. 285) notes that, in 1897, as a result of a resolution adopted by the AAPA, the National Society of Certified Public Accountants (NSCPA) was organized as a separate organization of CPAs. The NSCPA likely represented an effort by the AAPA to nationalize the CPA movement. For example, Webster (1954, p. 287) notes that "perhaps the greatest activity of the [NSCPA] was its efforts to have all [CPAs] become members." Miranti (1990, p. 59) notes that the NSCPA was "devoted to the promotion of CPA legislation." Webster (1954, pp. 286–289) suggests that the organization was relatively inactive. In fact, Webster (1954, pp. 288–290) suggests that, after the turn-of-the century, the organization became "dormant" (p. 290). However, Webster (1954, p. 290) notes

> on March 19, 1941 [NSCPA's] surviving members . . . transferred to the [American Institute of Accountants] the corporation, its name and the property thereto belonging. And with that action it was back where it was born.

The Federation

Webster (1954, p. 291) notes that, at the beginning of 1902, the AAPA was basically a "local" organization. Further, Webster (1954, p. 308) notes that at that time the AAPA "was planned to be a national society its membership and activities prior to 1897 made it practically a local organization." Thus, the time was right for a national organization. Such a national group was organized by George Wilkinson with the cooperation of the then existing state societies. This new national organization, the Federation of

Societies of Public Accountants in the United States of America (Federation), was organized at a 28 October 1902 meeting in Washington, D.C. (Webster, 1954, pp. 291–293). Webster (1954, p. 294) suggests that the Federation was becoming a national organization. Miranti (1990, p. 49) suggests that the Federation was organized to coordinate public accounting legislation. Miranti (1990, pp. 64–68) describes a series of events that eventually led to the combining of the AAPA and the Federation (also see Webster, 1954, p. 296). In 1905 the Federation consolidated with the AAPA and the consolidated organization continued as the AAPA (Webster, 1954, pp. 293, 317; History of AIA, 1938, pp. 8–10). Miranti (1990, p. 68) indicates that it was at this point that "the AAPA [had become] the national organization of the accounting profession. . . ."

AIA, ASCPA, and AICPA

In 1916 the AAPA reorganized under the name of the Institute of Accountants in the United States of America (History of AIA, 1938, p. 15). Due to the length of the new name, in 1917 the name was changed to the American Institute of Accountants (History of AIA, 1938, p. 15). However, with the new name, the American Institute of Accountants no longer required a CPA certificate as a prerequisite for membership (for example, Previts and Merino, 1979, pp. 148, 205). In 1921 this circumstance and other issues resulted in the American Society of Certified Public Accountants (ASCPA) being organized among those dissatisfied with AIA policies (see, for example, the discussion in Previts and Merino, 1979, pp. 205–209). Eventually, in 1936 the two organizations merged and kept the AIA's name (see, for example, Previts and Merino 1979, p. 255; Roberts, 1987, p. 42). In 1957 the AIA changed its name to the AICPA (Roberts, 1987, p. 42).

7 The IA's rooms (offices) are discussed in the next Section of our book. Also, there is an indication in "The Institute of Accounts" (1894, p. 184) that the IA's events held on 15 May 1894 were well attended and included members who for various reasons recently had not been active in the IA. Also, it appears that certain individuals who were likely IA members had sent "telegrams or letters of regret" ("The Institute of Accounts," 1894, p. 184). Apparently, Charles Cady "read" these messages after the dinner ("The Institute of Accounts," 1894, p. 184). More specifically

telegrams were in hand from Arthur Stonham, Philadelphia, and Hugo Schumacher, of Akron, O. Letters were read from Lewis C. Muzzy, Worcester, Mass.; Edward Gunster, Jr., Wilksbarre, Pa.; J.H. McNish, Boston, Mass.; George C. Darling, Wilcox, Pa., and J.W. Amerman, Texarkana, Tex.

("Institute of Accounts," 1894, p. 184)

It is likely that most if not all of these individuals were members of the IA and that they either temporarily or permanently were not in the New York City area. For example, a note in the July 1897 issue of *Accountics: A Monthly Magazine for Office Men* ("John W. Amermann. M.I.A.," 1897, p. 99) notes that a John W. Amermann of "Texarkana," "Texas" was "a member of the Institute of Accounts." It is likely that despite the slight difference in spelling of the last name it is the same individual mentioned in the preceding quote from 1894 ("The Institute of Accounts," 1894, p. 184). Also, later in our book we will discuss the IA nationalization in 1897. At the first "annual convention of the [nationalized] Institute of Accounts" one of the individuals elected "to serve one year" on the national "Executive Council" was "J.F. McNish, Boston, Mass" ("Convention of the Institute of Accounts," 1897, p. 66). It is likely that McNish's middle initial was "H." not "F." (see "Official Roster of Accountants' Associations," 1897a, 1897b).

8 Kingman (1952, p. 11) suggests that in 1896 the Massachusetts Institute of Accounts appears to have been formed in Boston and had likely evolved out of an earlier group – the Boston Bookkeepers' Association (also see Kistler, 1978, p. 155). An editorial in the July 1897 issue of *Accountics: A Monthly Magazine for Office Men* indicates that Clarence S. Anthony "was the first president of the Massachusetts Institute of Accounts" (Editorial, 1897, p. 98). Also, Kingman (1952, pp. 11–12) indicates that while the Massachusetts Institute of Accounts was viewed as a chapter of the National Institute of Accounts, evidence was not found that the Massachusetts Institute of Accounts existed beyond sometime in 1897. A note in the May 1898 issue of *Accountics: The Office Magazine* raises the possibility that the Massachusetts Institute of Accounts may have survived into 1898. More specifically, the note, which discusses what appears to be the May 20, 1898 meeting of the IA's New York chapter states that "a special guest of the chapter on this occasion, and one who participated in the discussion, was Charles Dyer Chase, of the Massachusetts Institute of Accounts, who formerly resided in the neighborhood of Boston,

but who is at present located in New York" ("New York Chapter," 1898, p. 45).

9 The IA's vice president, Albert Oscar Field, was office manager and chief accountant for and apparently had or was about to have an ownership "interest" in a clothing manufacturer ("Our Portraits," 1883, pp. 65–66). Thomas B. Conant, the IA's secretary, was employed in bookkeeping and also as "cashier and general manager" in a company dealing in plumbing supplies and other goods ("Our Portraits," 1883, p. 66). Joseph Rodgers, financial secretary of the association, was employed as the "cashier and general office-manager" for an international trading firm ("Our Portraits," 1883, pp. 66–67). And the IA's treasurer, Abraham Garrison, worked as a "book-keeper" at a manufacturer of "printing-ink" ("Our Portraits," 1883, p. 67). Also, see Loeb (2002a, p. 2; 2002c, p. 19).

10 In that work, clerk Bob Cratchit likely does not provide a strong image for accountants and bookkeepers (see, e.g., Dickens, 1995; also see Wescott and Seiler 1986, p. 6; Cory, 1992, pp. 3–4). More generally, see the discussion in Robert (1955, pp. 416–417; 1957 p. 65), Stacey (1958), and Bougen (1994, especially pp. 325–328).

11 As we discuss below, Charles W. Haskins, one of the individuals who established Haskins & Sells, was later drawn to and then joined the IA during the late 1890s and was involved in the establishment of NYU's SCAF, whose first faculty drew from the IA's membership including Charles W. Haskins, Charles Sprague, and Anson Kittredge (see, e.g., the discussion in Committee on History, 1953b, pp. 261–262).

12 The New York State Society of Certified Public Accountants not long after that association's founding established a service apparently relating to job recruitment (The Committee on History, 1954, p. 455).

13 The penchant for mathematics in economics had also been encouraged by the desire to follow the example of physics (see the discussion in Mirowski, 1989, chapter 1; also see the discussion in Cohen, 1994). McMillan (1998b, pp. 32, 42, 46; 1998c, pp. 18, 21) cite Mirowski (1989). McMillan (1998b, p. 32) also cites Mirowski (1994).

14 The annual number of individuals ("in thousands") graduating from high school in the U.S. increased from 24,000 in 1880, to 44,000 in 1890, and to 95,000 in 1900 (U.S. Bureau of the Census, 1975, p. 379). In 1890 high school graduates represented 3.5 percent of individuals aged 17, a percentage that increased to 6.3 percent by 1900 (U.S. Bureau of the Census, 1975, p. 379).

15 A note ("'Men Loved Darkness Rather Than Light, For Their

Deeds Were Evil'," 1901, p. 1) likely written by the editor of *Commerce, Accounts & Finance* suggested the need for corporate financial statements supported by audits conducted by independent CPAs. Further the note suggested that unless "industrial corporations" provided this on a voluntary basis, public policy makers might mandate such a system of governance ("'Men Loved Darkness Rather Than Light, For Their Deeds Were Evil.'," 1901, p. 1). Also see McMillan (1998b, chapter 7) for an in-depth discussion of auditing during the nineteenth century in Great Britain and the U.S.

16 At that time a committee consisting of Anson O. Kittredge, Alfred O. Field, and Charles Sprague drafted petitions (one of which included a suggested bill) to amend a state law that allowed borrowers three days of grace on the maturity date of "drafts, bills of exchange or promissory notes" ("Days of Grace," 1883, p. 49). From the perspective of the IA's advocates, the "days of grace" convention was archaic, originating in an era when U.S. "communication and transportation" were much more primitive than they had become by the 1880s ("Days of Grace," 1883, p. 49). In March 1883 "Assemblyman Theodore Roosevelt" "introduced" the IA's bill into the legislature (Notes from the Editors' Table, 1883, p. 108). Also, see the discussion in Romeo and Kyj (1998, p. 46).

17 Haskins (1901, p. 9) in an article published in *Commerce, Accounts & Finance* notes that "accountancy is a deep, broad science, demanding originative thought; a practical, progressive science, calling for the best adaptive talent." Haskins' view that accounting is a science also can be found in, for example, Haskins (1904a, 1904b, 1904c).

18 On the theoretical level Haskins' likely guide was his relative Ralph Waldo Emerson (see, e.g., "Haskins, Charles Waldo," 1907, p. 515); for more details on this point see Miranti (1988, p. 365; 1990, p. 37; 1993a, pp. ix–x). On the pragmatic level his guide likely was a relative of his wife, William F. Havemeyer, who among other things, was a New York City governmental leader and reformer (see, e.g., the discussion in "Haskins, Charles Waldo," 1907, p. 515; Miranti, 1990, p. 36; Mandelbaum, 1965, pp. 82–83, 93–95, 97–101).

19 It also may have been reflective of more general racial attitudes that existed during this era (see Wiebe, 1967, pp. 58–59).

20 The authorship of the IA's bill remains a controversial issue. George Wilkinson (1903, p. 414; 1928, p. 264) attributed authorship to Henry Harney in reminiscences that Webster (1954, p. 214) notes were likely written some years after the fact. Webster, however, after reconsideration of contemporary evidence,

disputes this conclusion, suggesting that the drafting of the bill likely was a collective activity primarily involving Sprague (Webster, 1954, pp. 215–217). Also see Loeb (2002c, p. 19; 2002e, p. 161).

21 See Miranti (1988, pp. 370–371; 1990, pp. 53–56; 1996, pp. 14–18) for a discussion of these events. Also see, e.g., Wilkinson (1903, pp. 414–416).

22 See note 6 and Figure 1.1.

23 See notes 6 and 31. Also see Figure 1.1.

24 Charles W. Haskins' wife was a Havemeyer – her family was both affluent and prominent (see, e.g., "Haskins, Charles Waldo," 1907, p. 515; Haskins & Sells, 1970, p. 4; Miranti, 1988, p. 367; 1990, p. 36; 1993a, p. viii; 1996, p. 15).

25 During this era, the existence of negative feeling toward Great Britain on the part of some Americans is noted by Campbell (1976, p. 220).

26 By the late 1890s a nexus appears to have developed between the IA and the National Association of Credit Men (NACM). Bankers had an obvious interest in efficient office methods and also in using financial statements for evaluating credit risk. This link was exemplified by the election of "James G. Cannon, Vice President of the Fourth National Bank, New York and retiring President of the" NACM to the national presidency of the IA ("Third Annual Convention of the Institute of Accounts," 1899, p. 139). Anson O. Kittredge, editor of *Accountics*, also provided extensive coverage of the activities of the NACM (Kittredge, 1899a, p. 4; 1899b, pp. 68–70; 1899c, p. 86; 1899d, pp. 115–116). In addition, Kittredge served "as secretary of the American Institute of Bank Clerks, the educational enterprise begun in 1900 by the American Bankers Association . . ." ("Anson O. Kittredge," 1903, p. 10).

27 See note 6. Also, see Webster (1954, pp. 291–295). The NYSSCPA withdrew from the Federation in June of 1904 (Webster, 1954, p. 295).

28 See note 6 and Figure 1.1.

29 See note 6 and Figure 1.1.

30 Also, see note 6 and Figure 1.1.

31 Webster (1954, p. 14) states that "the Institute [of Accounts] continued into the 20th century and on March 15, 1940 its two surviving members merged it into the American Institute of Accounts." Webster's comment is confirmed by the following note in the "Midyear Report" which was part of the "Reports of the Executive Committee" to AIA's Council and was published in the *1940 Yearbook of the American Institute of Accountants* ("Reports of the Executive Committee: Midyear Report," 1941, pp. 120–129):

The executive committee authorized counsel to take steps, if possible, to merge or associate with the Institute [AIA], the [NSCPA] and the Institute of Accounts, two older accounting organizations which have been inactive for many years, but of which a few members remain living, in order that it may be truly asserted that the present Institute is the successor of all recognized professional accounting organizations in the United States. The Institute of Accounts has now been merged with the Institute, and necessary steps to effect the merger of the National Society are being taken.

("Older Accounting Societies," 1941, p. 125)

Information could not be located to confirm the NSCPA's merger with the AIA in 1941. The earlier quote from Webster, however, indicates that the combination did occur (see note 6).

Webster (1954, pp. 9–17, 276–280) indicates that there were a number of other accounting or accounting-related associations in the nineteenth century and early twentieth century in the U.S. However, the AIA chose only two such organizations with which to associate – the NSCPA and the IA. The former organization was, in essence, created by the AAPA (see note 6).

The names of the two remaining members of the IA at the time of the 1940 merger with the AIA do not appear to be known. We feel, however, that the following evidence suggests that the two remaining IA members were possibly two of the following three individuals: Leonard Conant, Farquhar MacRae, and Frank Broaker. Webster (1954, p. 284) indicates that Conant and Broaker were members of both the NSCPA and the Institute of Accounts. Webster (1954) indicates that Broaker died in November of 1941 (p. 336) and Conant died in June of 1945 (p. 341). Both Broaker and Conant were past presidents of the AAPA (Carey 1969, pp. 374–375). Webster (1954, p. 362) notes that MacRae was a member of the IA, a founder of the NYSSCPAs, and in 1903 President of the Federation. Further, Webster (1954, p. 362) notes that MacRae died in 1947. Also, see the comment in Romeo and Kyj (2000, p. 132) about MacRae.

References

Abel, R.L. 1989. *American Lawyers*, New York: Oxford University Press.

Accountants' Index: A Bibliography of Accounting Literature to December, 1920, 1921. American Institute of Accountants. Reprinted in two volumes by Garland Publishing, Inc., New York, 1988.

"*Accountics: The Office Magazine,*" January 1900a. *Accountics: The Office Magazine,* 6: 7. Reprinted in *Accountics, April 1897 to August 1900,* Part III: Volumes VI and VII, January 1900 to August 1900, Garland Publishing, Inc., New York, 1992.

"*Accountics: The Office Magazine,*" August 1900b. *Accountics: The Office Magazine,* 7: 23. Reprinted in *Accountics, April 1897 to August 1900,* Part III: Volumes VI and VII, January 1900 to August 1900, Garland Publishing, Inc., New York, 1992.

"Accounting Guarantee Company," May 1897. *Accountics: A Monthly Magazine for Office Men,* 1: 44. Reprinted in *Accountics, April 1897 to August 1900,* Part I: Volumes I and II, April 1897 to March 1898, Garland Publishing, Inc., New York, 1992.

"Advertisement of 'The Book-Keeper.'," September 26, 1882. *The Book-Keeper.,* 5: 315. Reprinted in *The Book-Keeper and American Counting-Room,* Volume 2, January, 1882–June, 1883, Garland Publishing, Inc., New York, 1989.

Allen, D.G. and McDermott, K. 1993. *Accounting for Success: A History of Price Waterhouse in America, 1890–1990,* Boston: Harvard Business School Press.

"The American Association of Public Accountants," January 1899, *The Public Accountant,* 1: 40–41.

"Anson O. Kittredge," April 1903. *Commerce, Accounts & Finance*, 5: 9–10. Reprinted in *Commerce, Accounts & Finance*, Volume IV–V, January, 1902–May, 1903, New York: Garland Publishing, Inc., 1993.

Arrington, C.E. and Francis, J.R. 1989. "Letting the Chat Out of the Bag: Deconstruction, Privilege and Accounting Research," *Accounting, Organization and Society*, 14: 1–28.

"Bank Book-Keeping.," 1880–1881. *The Book-Keeper.* (August 31, 1880) 1: 49–50, (September 14, 1880) 1: 66, (September 28, 1880) 1: 83–85, (October 12, 1880) 1: 101–103, (October 26, 1880) 1: 116–117, (November 9, 1880) 1: 132–135, (November 23, 1880) 1: 146–149, (December 7, 1880) 1: 161–163, (December 21, 1880) 1: 180–182; (January 4, 1881) 2: 4–6, (January 18, 1881) 2: 20–22, (February 1, 1881) 2: 35–37, (February 15, 1881) 2: 51–54, (March 15, 1881) 2: 66–68, (April 12, 1881) 2: 82–85, (May 24, 1881) 2: 100–101, (June 7, 1881) 2: 116–118, (June 21, 1881) 2: 132–135, (July 5, 1881) 2: 149–151, (August 2, 1881) 2: 182–183; (August 30, 1881) 3: 20–22, (September 13, 1881) 3: 34–35, (September 27, 1881) 3: 54–55, (October 11, 1881) 3: 68–69, (November 8, 1881) 3: 100–103, (December 20, 1881) 3: 147–149. Reprinted in *The Book-Keeper and American Counting-Room*, Volume 1, July, 1880–December, 1881, Garland Publishing, Inc., New York, 1989.

Barrett, J.R. December 1992. "Americanization from the Bottom Up: Immigration and the Remaking of the Working Class in the United States, 1880–1930," *The Journal of American History*, 79: 996–1020.

Baskin, J.B. and Miranti, Jr., P.J. 1997. *A History of Corporate Finance*, Cambridge: Cambridge University Press.

Bedford, N.M. 1997. *A History of Accountancy at the University of Illinois at Urbana–Champaign*. Champaign, IL: Center for International Education and Research in Accounting, University of Illinois, Urbana–Champaign.

Board of Examiners of Public Accountants [New York]. May 11, 1897. "Minutes of the Board of Examiners of Public Accountants," pp. 29–31.

"The Book-keeper.," July 20, 1880a. *The Book-Keeper.*, 1: 8. Reprinted in *The Book-Keeper and American Counting-Room*, Volume 1, July, 1880–December, 1881, Garland Publishing, Inc., New York, 1989.

"The Book-keeper.," August 31, 1880b. *The Book-Keeper.*, 1: 56.

Reprinted in *The Book-Keeper and American Counting-Room*, Volume 1, July, 1880–December, 1881, Garland Publishing, Inc., New York, 1989.

"Book-keepers' Associations.," December 7, 1880. *The Book-Keeper.*, 1: 166. Reprinted in *The Book-Keeper and American Counting-Room*, Volume 1, July, 1880–December, 1881, Garland Publishing, Inc., New York, 1989.

"Book-keepers' Associations and Employers.," February 1, 1881. *The Book-Keeper.*, 2: 40–41. Reprinted in *The Book-Keeper and American Counting-Room*, Volume 1, July, 1880–December, 1881, Garland Publishing, Inc., New York, 1989.

Bougen, P.D. 1994. "Joking Apart: The Serious Side to the Accountant Stereotype," *Accounting, Organizations and Society*, 19: 319–335.

Brief, R.P. Spring 1965. "Nineteenth Century Accounting Error," *Journal of Accounting Research*, 3: 12–31.

"Brooklyn Chapter," March 1898a. *Accountics: The Office Magazine* 2: 124. Reprinted in *Accountics, April 1897 to August 1900*, Part I: Volumes I and II, April 1897 to March 1898, Garland Publishing, Inc., New York, 1992.

"Brooklyn Chapter," May 1898b. *Accountics: The Office Magazine,* 3: 45. Reprinted in *Accountics, April 1897 to August 1900*, Part II: Volumes III, IV and V, April 1898 to December 1899, Garland Publishing, Inc., New York, 1992.

Burrow, J.G. 1977. *Organized Medicine in the Progressive Era: The Move Toward Monopoly*, Baltimore: The Johns Hopkins University Press.

Cady, C.E. September 1891. "The Value and Importance of the Institute of Accounts.," *The Office: A Practical Journal of Business*, 11: 189–190.

Calhoun, D.H. 1960. *The American Civil Engineer: Origins and Conflict*, Cambridge, MA: The Technology Press, Massachusetts Institute of Technology.

Calvert, M.A. 1967. *The Mechanical Engineer in America, 1830–1910: Professional Cultures in Conflict*, Baltimore: The Johns Hopkins University Press.

Campbell, C.S. 1976. *The Transformation of American Foreign Relations, 1865–1900*, New York: Harper & Row Publishers.

"'Is Capital Account a Liability?'," December 19, 1882. *The Book-Keeper.*, 5: 397–398. Reprinted in *The Book-Keeper and American Counting-Room*, Volume 2, January, 1882–June, 1883, Garland Publishing, Inc., New York, 1989.

Caplow, T. 1954. *The Sociology of Work*, Minneapolis: University of Minnesota.

Carey, J.L. 1969. *The Rise of the Accounting Profession: From Technician to Professional, 1996–1936*, New York: American Institute of Certified Public Accountants.

Carnegie, G.D. March 1993. "The Australian Institute of Incorporated Accountants (1892–1938)," *Accounting, Business & Financial History*, 3: 61–80.

Chandler, A.D., Jr. 1977. *The Visible Hand: The Managerial Revolution in American Business*, Cambridge, MA: Harvard University Press.

"Change of Name.," July 1886. *The Office: A Practical Journal for Business Managers, Accountants and Office Men.*, 1: 30.

"Changing from a Partnership to a Corporation.," June 5, 1883. *The Book-Keeper.*, 6: 177–179. Reprinted in *The Book-Keeper and American Counting-Room*, Volume 2, January, 1882–June, 1883, Garland Publishing, Inc., New York, 1989.

"Charles Dutton, F.I.A.," April 1897. *Accountics: A Monthly Magazine for Office Men*, 1: 20. Reprinted in *Accountics, April 1897 to August 1900*, Part I: Volumes I and II, April 1897 to March 1898, Garland Publishing, Inc., New York, 1992.

"Charles E. Sprague, Ph.D.," September 1897. *Accountics: A Monthly Magazine for Office Men*, 1: 129. Reprinted in *Accountics, April 1897 to August 1900*, Part I: Volumes I and II, April 1897 to March 1898, Garland Publishing, Inc., New York, 1992.

Chatfield, M. 1974. *A History of Accounting Thought*, Hinsdale, IL: The Dryden Press.

Chatfield, M. 1996a. "Entity Theory," in M. Chatfield and R. Vangermeersch, eds, *The History of Accounting: An International Encyclopedia*, New York: Garland Publishing, Inc., pp. 230–231.

Chatfield, M. 1996b. "Proprietary Theory," in M. Chatfield and R. Vangermeersch, eds, *The History of Accounting: An International Encyclopedia*, New York: Garland Publishing, Inc., pp. 479–481.

"Chicago Society of Accountants," September 1897. *Accountics: A Monthly Magazine for Office Men*, 1: 143. Reprinted in *Accountics, April 1897 to August 1900*, Part I: Volumes I and II, April 1897 to March 1898, Garland Publishing, Inc., New York, 1992.

Clarke, S.N. June 1902. "The Lawyer and the Accountant," *Commerce, Accounts & Finance*, 4: 17. Reprinted in *Commerce, Accounts & Finance*, Volume IV–V, January, 1902–May, 1903, New York: Garland Publishing, Inc., 1993.

Clemens, G. June 6, 1882. "Entry in Partnership Accounts.," *The Book-Keeper.*, 4: 182. Reprinted in *The Book-Keeper and American Counting-Room*, Volume 2, January, 1882–June, 1883, Garland Publishing, Inc., New York, 1989.

Cohen, I.B. 1994. "Newton and the Social Sciences, with Special Reference to Economics, or, the Case of the Missing Paradigm," in P. Mirowski, ed., *Natural Images in Economic Thought: "Markets Read in Tooth and Claw*," Cambridge: Cambridge University Press, pp. 55–90.

Collins, R. 1979. *The Credential Society: An Historical Sociology of Education and Stratification*, New York: Academic Press.

The Committee on History. May 1949. "The New York State Society of Certified Public Accountants: Its Genesis," *The New York Certified Public Accountant*, 19: 327, 329.

The Committee on History. September 1951. "Joseph Hardcastle," *The New York Certified Public Accountant*, 21: 615–618.

The Committee on History. July 1952. "Charles Ezra Sprague – Public Accountant," *The New York Certified Public Accountant*, 22: 430–432.

Committee on History. March 1953a. "The Incorporators of the New York State Society of Certified Public Accountants," *The New York Certified Public Accountant*, 23: 217–221, 232.

Committee on History. April 1953b. "The School of Commerce, Accounts, and Finance of New York University – Its Promotion and Organization," *The New York Certified Public Accountant*, 23: 260–262.

The Committee on History. July 1954. "Society Offices and Secretarial Staff," *The New York Certified Public Accountant*, 24: 454–461.

"Compensation vs. Services.," June 21, 1881. *The Book-Keeper.*, 2: 136–137. Reprinted in *The Book-Keeper and American Counting-Room*, Volume 1, July, 1880–December, 1881, Garland Publishing, Inc., New York, 1989.

"Convention of the Institute of Accounts," June 1897. *Accountics: A Monthly Magazine for Office Men*, 1: 66. Reprinted in *Accountics, April 1897 to August 1900*, Part I: Volumes I and II, April 1897 to March 1898, Garland Publishing, Inc., New York, 1992.

"Convention of the Institute of Accounts," June 1900. *Accountics: The Office Magazine*, 6: 88. Reprinted in *Accountics, April 1897 to August 1900*, Part III: Volumes VI and VII, January 1900 to August 1900, Garland Publishing, Inc., New York, 1992.

Corning, R.R. August 15, 1882. "Entry in Partnership Accounts.," *The Book-Keeper.*, 5: 259–260. Reprinted in *The Book-Keeper and American Counting-Room*, Volume 2, January, 1882–June, 1883, Garland Publishing, Inc., New York, 1989.

Cory, S.N. Spring 1992. "Quality and Quantity of Accounting Students and the Stereotypical Accountant: Is There a Relationship?," *Journal of Accounting Education*, 10: 1–24.

Curti, M. 1964. *The Growth of American Thought*, Third Edition, New York: Harper & Row, Publishers.

Curtis, G.T. April/May/June 1884. "Legal-Tender Paper Money.," *American Counting-room.*, 8: 214–223. Reprinted in *The Book-Keeper and American Counting-Room*, Volume 4, January, 1884–December, 1884, Garland Publishing, Inc., New York, 1989.

"Days of Grace.," February 13, 1883. *The Book-Keeper.*, 6: 49–50. Reprinted in *The Book-Keeper and American Counting-Room*, Volume 2, January, 1882–June, 1883, Garland Publishing, Inc., New York, 1989.

"'Debit' and 'Credit'.," December 5, 1882. *The Book-Keeper.*, 5: 381–383. Reprinted in *The Book-Keeper and American Counting-Room*, Volume 2, January, 1882–June, 1883, Garland Publishing, Inc., New York, 1989.

"Decisions in Commercial Law,.," 1882. *The Book-Keeper.* (October 24) 5: 343, (November 7) 5: 355–356, (November 21) 5: 373–374. Reprinted in *The Book-Keeper and American Counting-Room*, Volume 2, January, 1882–June, 1883, Garland Publishing, Inc., New York, 1989.

Dickens, C. 1995. *A Christmas Carol*, New York: Bantam Books, Fourth Bantam Reissue.

Donderundblitzen, H. [pseud.]. March 27, 1883. "Examintionserfahrungen Eines Neuen Mitgliedes.," *The Book-Keeper.*, 6: 103–104. Reprinted in *The Book-Keeper and American Counting-Room*, Volume 2, January, 1882–June, 1883, Garland Publishing, Inc., New York, 1989.

Dutton, C. April 1897. "The Vital Element of Business," *Accountics: A Monthly Magazine for Office Men* 1: 1–6. Reprinted in *Accountics, April 1897 to August 1900*, Part I: Volumes I and II, April 1897 to March 1898, Garland Publishing, Inc., New York, 1992.

Editorial. July 1897. *Accountics: A Monthly Magazine for Office Men*, 1: 98. Reprinted in *Accountics, April 1897 to August 1900*, Part I:

Volumes I and II, April 1897 to March 1898, Garland Publishing, Inc., New York, 1992.

"Edward C. Cockey.," January 30, 1883. *The Book-Keeper.*, 6: 33–34. Reprinted in *The Book-Keeper and American Counting-Room*, Volume 2, January, 1882–June, 1883, Garland Publishing, Inc., New York, 1989.

Edwards, J.D. 1960. *History of Public Accounting in the United States*, East Lansing: Bureau of Business and Economic Research, Graduate School of Business Administration, Michigan State University.

"Examinations for Membership in the Institute.," October 24, 1882. *The Book-Keeper.*, 5: 338. Reprinted in *The Book-Keeper and American Counting-Room*, Volume 2, January, 1882–June, 1883, Garland Publishing, Inc., New York, 1989.

"Favoring a National Institute.," November 1883. *American Counting-room.*, 7: 293–294. Reprinted in *The Book-Keeper and American Counting-Room*, Volume 3, July, 1883–December, 1883, Garland Publishing, Inc., 1989.

"The First Annual Meeting of the Institute of Accountants and Book-keepers of the City of New York.," March 27, 1883. *The Book-Keeper.* 6: 97–98. Reprinted in *The Book-Keeper and American Counting-Room*, Volume 2, January, 1882–June, 1883, Garland Publishing, Inc., New York, 1989.

"First Fall Meeting of the Institute.," September 26, 1882. *The Book-Keeper.*, 5: 302. Reprinted in *The Book-Keeper and American Counting-Room*, Volume 2, January, 1882–June, 1883, Garland Publishing, Inc., New York, 1989.

Fleischman, R.K., Parker, L.D., and Vamplew, W. 1991. "New Cost Accounting Perspectives on Technological Change in the British Industrial Revolution," in O. Finley Graves, ed., *The Costing Heritage: Studies in Honor of S. Paul Garner*, (Monograph 6) Harrisonburg, VA, The Academy of Accounting Historians, pp. 11–24.

Flesher, D.L. and Flesher, T.K. July 1986. "Ivar Krueger's Contribution to U.S. Financial Reporting," *The Accounting Review*, 61: 421–434.

Flesher, D.L., Flesher, T.K., and Previts, G.J. April 1996. "Joseph Hardcastle: The First Person to Pass the CPA Exam," *The CPA Journal*, 66: 16–17.

Flesher, D.L., Miranti, P.J., and Previts, G.J. October 1996. "The First Century of the CPA," *Journal of Accountancy*, 182: 51–57.

Foucault, M. 1972. *The Archaeology of Knowledge* (A.M. Sheridan Smith, trans.), New York: Pantheon Books.

Foucault, M. 1973a. *Madness and Civilization: A History of Insanity in the Age of Reason* (R. Howard, trans.), New York: Vintage Books.

Foucault, M. 1973b. *The Order of Things: An Archaeology of Human Sciences*, New York: Vintage Books.

Foucault, M. 1979. *Discipline and Punish: The Birth of the Prison* (A. Sheridan, trans.), New York: Vintage Books.

Gabriel, R.H. with Walker, R.H. 1986. *The Course of American Democratic Thought*, Third Edition, Contribution to American Studies 87, New York: Greenwood Press.

Galambos, L. n.d. *America at Middle Age: A New History of the United States in the Twentieth Century*, New York: McGraw-Hill Book Company.

Galambos, L. Winter 1983. "Technology, Political Economy, and Professionalization: Central Themes of Organizational Synthesis," *Business History Review*, 57: 471–493.

Galambos, L. and Pratt, J. 1988. *The Rise of the Corporate Commonwealth: U.S. Business and Public Policy in the Twentieth Century*, New York: Basic Books, Inc., Publishers.

Garner, S.P. 1954. *Evolution of Cost Accounting to 1925*, University, Alabama: University of Alabama Press.

Gerstle, G. September 1997. "Liberty, Coercion, and the Making of Americans," *The Journal of American History*, 84: 524–558.

Gordon, R.W. 1983. "Legal Thought and Legal Practice in the Age of American Enterprise, 1870–1920," in G.L. Geison, ed., *Professions and Professional Ideologies in America*, Chapel Hill: The University of North Carolina Press, pp. 70–110.

Guthrie, W.K.C. 1971. *A History of Greek Philosophy: Volume I, The Earlier Presocratics and the Pythagoreans*, Cambridge: Cambridge University Press.

Hammond, T.A. 2002. *A White-Collar Profession: African American Certified Public Accountants Since 1921*, Chapel Hill: The University of North Carolina Press.

Hardcastle, J. 1883a. "Equation of Payments Mathematically Considered. First Theoretical.," *American Counting-room.* (October) 7: 219–222, and (November) "Equation of Payments Mathematically Considered. Second – Practical.," 7: 281–286. Reprinted in *The Book-Keeper and American Counting-Room*, Volume 3, July, 1883–December, 1883, Garland Publishing, Inc., New York, 1989.

Hardcastle, J. 1883b. "On the Theory of Life Insurance.," *The Book-Keeper.* (January 16) 6: 17–20, (January 30) 6: 35–37. Reprinted in

The Book-Keeper and American Counting-Room, Volume 2, January, 1882–June, 1883, Garland Publishing, Inc., New York, 1989.

Hardcastle, J. March 1884. "Calculating Interest on Bonds.," *American Counting-room.*, 8: 155–157. Reprinted in *The Book-Keeper and American Counting-Room*, Volume 4, January, 1884–December, 1884, Garland Publishing, Inc., New York, 1989.

Hardcastle, J. November 1888. "Distribution of the Income of Building and Loan Associations.," *The Office: A Practical Journal of Business Management, Office Routine and Art of Advertising.*, 5: 225–228.

Hardcastle, J. March 1889a. "The Principles on which a Building and Loan Association Should Be Founded.," *The Office: A Practical Journal of Business Management, Office Routine and Art of Advertising.*, 6: 43–44.

Hardcastle, J. October 1889b. "Cooperative Building and Loan Associations.," *The Office: A Practical Journal of Business Management, Office Routine and Art of Advertising.*, 7: 180–183.

Hardcastle, J. July 1897a. "Logismography – I," *Business: The Office Paper*, 17: 203–204.

Hardcastle, J. August 1897b. "Logismography – II," *Business: The Office Paper*, 17: 235–236.

Hardcastle, J. September 1897c. "Logismography – III," *Business: The Office Paper*, 17: 273–275.

Hardcastle, J. October 1897d. "Logismography – IV, (Fire Insurance)," *Business: The Office Paper*, 17: 303–304.

Hardcastle, J. November 1897e. "Logismography – V, (Fire Insurance)," *Business: The Office Paper*, 17: 335–337.

Hardcastle, J. December 1897f. "Logismography – VI, (Fire Insurance)," *Business: The Office Paper*, 17: 366–370.

Hardcastle, J. January 1903a. "Bonds as Investments," *Commerce, Accounts & Finance*, 5: 8–9. Reprinted in *Commerce, Accounts & Finance*, Volume IV–V, January, 1902–May, 1903, New York: Garland Publishing, Inc., 1993.

Hardcastle, J. March 1903b. "Interest," *Commerce, Accounts & Finance*, 5: 13–15. Reprinted in *Commerce, Accounts & Finance*, Volume IV–V, January, 1902–May, 1903, New York: Garland Publishing, Inc., 1993.

"Hartford Chapter," March 1898a. *Accountics: The Office Magazine*, 2: 124. Reprinted in *Accountics, April 1897 to August 1900*, Part I:

Volumes I and II, April 1897 to March 1898, Garland Publishing, Inc., New York, 1992.

"Hartford Chapter," April 1898b. *Accountics: The Office Magazine*, 3: 3–6. Reprinted in *Accountics, April 1897 to August 1900*, Part II: Volumes III, IV and V, April 1898 to December 1899, Garland Publishing, Inc., New York, 1992.

"Hartford Chapter of the Institute of Accounts," September 1899. *Accountics: The Office Magazine*, 5: 52–53. Reprinted in *Accountics, April 1897 to August 1900*, Part II: Volumes III, IV and V, April 1898 to December 1899, Garland Publishing, Inc., New York, 1992.

Haskell, T.L. 1977. *The Emergence of Professional Social Science: The American Social Science Association and the Nineteenth-Century Crisis of Authority*, Urbana: University of Illinois Press.

Haskins, C.W. 1900a. "Accounting: Its Present and Its Past," *Accountics*, (March) 6: 33–34, (April) 6: 51, (May) 6: 69–70. Reprinted in *Accountics: The Office Magazine, April 1897 to August 1900*, Part III: Volumes VI and VII, January 1900 to August 1900, Garland Publishing, Inc., New York, 1992.

Haskins, C.W. September 1900b. "School of Commerce, Accounts, and Finance of New York University," *Business: The Office Paper and the Public Accountant*, 20: 409–412.

Haskins, C.W. January 19, 1901. "Congratulatory – 'Commerce, Accounts and Finance,'" *Commerce, Accounts & Finance*, 1: 9. Reprinted in *Commerce, Accounts & Finance*, Volume I–III, January–December 1901, New York: Garland Publishing, Inc., 1993.

Haskins, C.W. 1904a. "The Possibilities of the Profession of Accountancy as a Moral and Educational Force," in C.W. Haskins (edited by F.A. Cleveland), *Business Education and Accountancy*, New York: Harper & Brothers Publishers, pp. 90–109.

Haskins, C.W. 1904b. "The Growing Need for Higher Accountancy," in C.W. Haskins (edited by F.A. Cleveland), *Business Education and Accountancy*, New York: Harper & Brothers Publishers, pp. 110–125.

Haskins, C.W. 1904c. "The Place of the Science of Accounts in Collegiate Commercial Education," in C.W. Haskins (edited by F.A. Cleveland), *Business Education and Accountancy*, New York: Harper & Brothers Publishers, pp. 126–137.

"Haskins, Charles Waldo," 1907. In *The National Cyclopaedia of American Biography*, Volume IX, New York: John T. White & Company, pp. 514–515.

Haskins & Sells. 1970. *Haskins & Sells: Our First Seventy-Five Years*, reprinted by Garland Publishing, Inc, 1984.

Hays, S.P. 1957. *The Response to Industrialism: 1885–1914*, Chicago: The University of Chicago Press.

Herrick, M.T. 1923. "University Training for Business Men," in *Charles Waldo Haskins: An American Pioneer in Accountancy*, New York, Prentice Hall, Inc., pp. 91–100.

Higham, J. 1955. *Strangers in the Land: Patterns of American Nativism, 1860–1925*, New Brunswick, N.J., Rutgers University Press.

"A History of the American Institute of Accountants" (History of AIA), 1938. In *The American Institutes of Accountants (1887–1937), Fiftieth Anniversary Celebration 1937, October Eighteenth to Twenty-second*, American Institute of Accountants, pp. 3–29.

Hopkins, S.R. 1883. "The Organization and Classification of Accounts.," *The Book-Keeper.* (April 24) 6: 129–131, (May 8) 6: 147–149. Reprinted in *The Book-Keeper and American Counting-Room*, Volume 2, January, 1882–June, 1883, Garland Publishing, Inc., New York, 1989.

Hopkins, S.R. 1883, 1884. "Public Moneys and Accounts.," *American Counting-room.* (November) 7: 261–263, (December) 7: 326–330; (January) 8: 4–8, (March) 8: 139–140. Reprinted in *The Book-Keeper and American Counting-Room*, Volume 3, July, 1883–December, 1883 and Volume 4, January, 1884–December, 1884, Garland Publishing, Inc., New York, 1989.

Horne, H.A. 1947. "The History and Administration of Our Society," in E. Saxe, Managing Editor, *The New York State Society of Certified Public Accountants, 1897–1947: Fiftieth Anniversary of the Founding of The New York State Society of Certified Public Accountants*, New York: The New York State Society of Certified Public Accountants, pp. 5–14.

Howitt, Sir H. 1966. *The History of the Institute of Chartered Accountants in England and Wales, 1880–1965, and of Its Founder Accountancy Bodies, 1870–1880: The Growth of a Profession and Its Influence on Legislation and Public Affairs*, London: William Heinemann, Ltd. Reprinted by Garland Publishing, Inc., New York, 1984, under the title *The History of the Institute of Chartered Accountants in England and Wales, 1870–1965*.

"Illinois Institute of Accountants," July 1898. *Accountics: The Office*

Magazine, 3: 89. Reprinted in *Accountics, April 1897 to August 1900*, Part II: Volumes III, IV and V, April 1898 to December 1899, Garland Publishing, Inc., New York, 1992.

"Illinois Institute of Accountants," November 1899. *Accountics: The Office Magazine*, 5: 89–90. Reprinted in *Accountics, April 1897 to August 1900*, Part II: Volumes III, IV and V, April 1898 to December 1899, Garland Publishing, Inc., New York, 1992.

"The Institute of Accounts.," February 1887. *The Office: A Practical Journal for Business Managers, Accountants and Office Men.*, 2: 29.

"The Institute of Accounts," September 1893. *Business: A Practical Journal of the Office*, 13: 321–322.

"The Institute of Accounts," May 1894. *Business: A Practical Journal of the Office*, 14: 184–185.

"The Institute of Accounts," February 1897. *Business: The Office Paper*, 17: 54.

"Institute of Accountants and Book-keepers.," June 6, 1882a. *The Book-Keeper.*, 4: 173. Reprinted in *The Book-Keeper and American Counting-Room*, Volume 2, January, 1882–June, 1883, Garland Publishing, Inc., New York, 1989.

"Institute of Accountants and Book-keepers.," June 20, 1882b. *The Book-Keeper.*, 4: 189–192. Reprinted in *The Book-Keeper and American Counting-Room*, Volume 2, January, 1882–June, 1883, Garland Publishing, Inc., New York, 1989.

"Institute of Accountants and Book-keepers of the City of New York.," August 1, 1882. *The Book-Keeper.*, 5: 248. Reprinted in *The Book-Keeper and American Counting-Room*, Volume 2, January, 1882–June, 1883, Garland Publishing, Inc., New York, 1989.

"Institute of Accounts.," October 1886a. *The Office: A Practical Journal for Business Managers, Accountants and Office Men.*, 1: 84.

"Institute of Accounts.," November 1886b. *The Office: A Practical Journal for Business Managers, Accountants and Office Men.*, 1: 104–105.

"Institute of Accounts.," January 1888a. *The Office: A Practical Journal of Business Management, Office Routine and the Art of Advertising.*, 4: vi.

"Institute of Accounts.," March 1888b. *The Office: A Practical Journal of Business Management, Office Routine and the Art of Advertising.*, 4: 48–50.

"Institute of Accounts.," July 1889. *The Office: A Practical Journal of*

Business Management, Office Routine and the Art of Advertising., 7: 138.

"Institute of Accounts.," November 1891. *Business: A Practical Journal of the Office*, 11: 238–240.

"Institute of Accounts," June 1896. *Business: The Office Paper* (121): 259–260.

"Institute of Accounts (National)," July 1897. *Accountics: A Monthly Magazine for Office Men*, 1: 100. Reprinted in *Accountics, April 1897 to August 1900*, Part I: Volumes I and II, April 1897 to March 1898, Garland Publishing, Inc., New York, 1992.

"Institute of Accounts, New York.," March 1887. *The Office: A Practical Journal for Business Managers, Accountants and Office Men.*, 2: 51–52.

"Institute News.," May 8, 1883. *The Book-Keeper.*, 6: 154–156. Reprinted in *The Book-Keeper and American Counting-Room*, Volume 2, January, 1882–June, 1883, Garland Publishing, Inc., New York, 1989.

Jaudon, W.B. May 1897. "Surrogate's Practice and the Accountant's Relation Thereto," *Accountics: A Monthly Magazine for Office Men*, 1: 27–35. Reprinted in *Accountics, April 1897 to August 1900*, Part I: Volumes I and II, April 1897 to March 1898, Garland Publishing, Inc., New York, 1992.

"John W. Amermann. M.I.A.," July 1897. *Accountics: A Monthly Magazine for Office Men*, 1: 99. Reprinted in *Accountics, April 1897 to August 1900*, Part I: Volumes I and II, April 1897 to March 1898, Garland Publishing, Inc., New York, 1992.

Johnson, H.T. and Kaplan, R.S. 1987. *Relevance Lost: The Rise and Fall of Management Accounting*, Boston: Harvard Business School Press.

Johnson, J.F. February 1902. "The Relation of Economics to Higher Accountancy," *Commerce, Accounts & Finance*, 4: 6–9. Reprinted in *Commerce, Accounts & Finance*, Volume IV–V, January, 1902–May, 1903, New York: Garland Publishing, Inc., 1993.

"Joint-Stock Book-keeping.," June 7, 1881. *The Book-Keeper.*, 2: 113–114. Reprinted in *The Book-Keeper and American Counting-Room*, Volume 1, July, 1880–December, 1881, Garland Publishing, Inc., New York, 1989.

Jones, E. 1981. *Accountancy and the British Economy, 1840–1980: The Evolution of Ernst & Whinney*, London: B.T. Batsford Ltd.

Jordan, W.G. 1923. "Biographical Sketch," in *Charles Waldo*

Haskins: An American Pioneer in Accountancy, New York: Prentice Hall, Inc., pp. 1–87.

Kelley, P. [pseud.]. August 15, 1882. "Pat Kelley's Examination.," *The Book-Keeper.*, 5: 256–257. Reprinted in *The Book-Keeper and American Counting-Room*, Volume 2, January, 1882–June, 1883, Garland Publishing, Inc., New York, 1989.

Kett, J.F. 1968. *The Formation of the American Medical Profession: The Role of Institutions, 1780–1860*, New Haven: Yale University Press.

Keys, R.B. 1884. "Building and Loan Associations.," *American Counting-room.* (February) 8 (I.): 65–70; (March) 8 (Article II.): 134–138; (April, May, June) 8 (Article III.): 204–209. Reprinted in *The Book-Keeper and American Counting-Room*, Volume 4, January, 1884–December, 1884, Garland Publishing, Inc., New York, 1989.

Kingman, E.S. 1952. *Accountancy in Massachusetts: A Brief Study*, Massachusetts Society of Certified Public Accountants, Inc.

Kistler, L.H. 1978. "Early Public Accountancy in Massachusetts," in W. Holmes, L.H. Kistler, and L.S. Corsini, *Three Centuries of Accounting in Massachusetts*, The Massachusetts Society of Certified Public Accountants, Inc., New York: Arno Press Inc.

Kittredge, A.O. "Foundry Book-keeping.," 1880. *The Book-Keeper.* (October 26) 1: 113–115; (November 9) 1: 130–132. Reprinted in *The Book-Keeper and American Counting-Room*, Volume 1, July, 1880–December, 1881, Garland Publishing, Inc., New York, 1989.

Kittredge, A.O. December 1897. "The Balance Sheet Ledger," *Accountics: A Monthly Magazine for Office Men*, 2: 48–68. Reprinted in *Accountics, April 1897 to August 1900*, Part I: Volumes I and II, April 1897 to March 1898, Garland Publishing, Inc., New York, 1992.

Kittredge, A.O. July 1899a. "The National Association of Credit Men," *Accountics: The Office Magazine*, 5: 4. Reprinted in *Accountics, April 1897 to August 1900*, Part II: Volumes III, IV and V, April 1898 to December 1899, Garland Publishing, Inc., New York, 1992.

Kittredge, A.O. October 1899b. "Credit Men's Affairs," *Accountics: The Office Magazine*, 5: 68–70. Reprinted in *Accountics, April 1897 to August 1900*, Part II: Volumes III, IV and V, April 1898 to December 1899, Garland Publishing, Inc., New York, 1992.

Kittredge, A.O. November 1899c. "Credit Men's Affairs," *Accountics:*

The Office Magazine, 5: 86. Reprinted in *Accountics, April 1897 to August 1900*, Part II: Volumes III, IV and V, April 1898 to December 1899, Garland Publishing, Inc., New York, 1992.

Kittredge, A.O. December 1899d. "Credit Men's Affairs," *Accountics: The Office Magazine*, 5: 115–116. Reprinted in *Accountics, April 1897 to August 1900*, Part II: Volumes III, IV and V, April 1898 to December 1899, Garland Publishing, Inc., New York, 1992.

Kittredge, A.O. 1900. "The Application of Advanced Accounting Methods to Modern Business Enterprises: II. The Cotton Mill," *Accountics: The Office Magazine*, (May) 6: 65–66, (June) 6: 81–82. Reprinted in *Accountics, April 1897 to August 1900*, Part III: Volumes VI and VII, January 1900 to August 1900, Garland Publishing, Inc., New York, 1992.

Kittredge, A.O. January 1903. "The Investigation and Audit of Trust Companies," *Commerce, Accounts & Finance*, 5: 5–7. Reprinted in *Commerce, Accounts & Finance*, Volume IV–V, January, 1902–May, 1903, New York: Garland Publishing, Inc., 1993.

Knights, D. and Collinson, D. 1987. "Disciplining the Shopfloor: A Comparison of the Disciplinary Effects on Managerial Psychology and Financial Accounting," *Accounting, Organization and Society*, 12: 457–477.

Kohler, R.E. 1982. *From Medical Chemistry to Biochemistry: The Making of a Biomedical Discipline*, Cambridge: Cambridge University Press.

Kohlstedt, S.G. 1976. *The Formation of the American Scientific Community: The American Association for the Advancement of Science, 1848–60*, Urbana: University of Illinois Press.

Korman, G. April 1965. "Americanization at the Factory Gate," *Industrial and Labor Relations Review*, 18: 396–419.

Kraines, O. September 1954. "The Dockery–Cockrell Commission, 1893–1895," *The Western Political Quarterly*, 7: 417–462.

Kyj, L.S. and Romeo, G.C. June 1997. "Paving the Way for the NYSSCPA: The Institute of Accounts," *The CPA Journal*, 67: 11, 15.

Lamoreaux, N.R. 1985. *The Great Merger Movement in American Business, 1895–1904*, Cambridge: Cambridge University Press.

Langenderfer, H.Q. May 1987. "Accounting Education's History – A 100-Year Search for Identity," *Journal of Accountancy*, 163: 302–308, 310–312, 314–315, 318, 320, 322–324, 326–331.

Lee, T.A. 1995. "The Professionalization of Accountancy: A History of Protecting the Public Interest in a Self-Interested Way," *Accounting, Auditing & Accountability Journal*, 8: 48–69.

Lehman, C.R. 1992. *Accounting's Changing Role in Social Conflict*, New York: Markus Wiener Publishing, Inc.; London: Paul Chapman Publishing.

Levenstein, M. 1991. "The Use of Cost Measures: The Dow Chemical Company, 1890–1914," in P. Temin, ed., *Inside the Business Enterprise: Historical Perspectives on the Use of Information*, Chicago: The University of Chicago Press, pp. 71–112.

Lipartito, K. Autumn 1990. "What Have Lawyers Done for American Business? The Case of Baker & Botts of Houston," *Business History Review*, 64: 489–526.

Lipartito, K.J. and Miranti, Jr., P.J. 1996. "The Professions," in S.I. Kutler, Editor-in-Chief, R. Dallek, D.A. Hollinger, and T.K. McCraw, Associate Editors, and J. Kirkwood, Assistant Editor, *Encyclopedia of The United States in the Twentieth Century, Volume III*, New York, Charles Scribner's Sons, Macmillan Library Reference USA, Simon & Schuster Macmillan; London: Simon & Schuster and Prentice Hall International, pp. 1407–1430.

Lipartito, K.J. and Miranti, P.J. 1998. "Professions and Organizations in Twentieth-Century America," *Social Science Quarterly*, 79: 301–320.

Loeb, S.E. 2002a. "Accounting in Maryland before 1899," in S.E. Loeb, Editor and E.A. Braase, Assistant Editor, *Our Past, Our Future – 100 Years of CPAs in Maryland: Maryland Association of Certified Public Accountants, Inc., 1901–2001*, Lutherville, MD, Maryland Association of Certified Public Accountants, Inc., pp. 1–8.

Loeb, S.E. 2002b. "The Founding of the Maryland CPA Profession," in S.E. Loeb, Editor and E.A. Braase, Assistant Editor, *Our Past, Our Future – 100 Years of CPAs in Maryland: Maryland Association of Certified Public Accountants, Inc., 1901–2001*, Lutherville, MD, Maryland Association of Certified Public Accountants, Inc., pp. 9–18.

Loeb, S.E. 2002c. "Early Maryland Accountants," in S.E. Loeb, Editor and E.A. Braase, Assistant Editor, *Our Past, Our Future – 100 Years of CPAs in Maryland: Maryland Association of Certified Public Accountants, Inc., 1901–2001*, Lutherville, MD, Maryland Association of Certified Public Accountants, Inc., pp. 19–27.

Loeb, S.E. 2002d. "The Beginning of Growth and Rise of the Multi-Person Firms: 1923–1956," in S.E. Loeb, Editor and E.A. Braase,

Assistant Editor, *Our Past, Our Future – 100 Years of CPAs in Maryland: Maryland Association of Certified Public Accountants, Inc., 1901–2001*, Lutherville, MD, Maryland Association of Certified Public Accountants, Inc., pp. 45–59.

Loeb, S.E. 2002e. "Conclusions and Beginning," in S.E. Loeb, Editor and E.A. Braase, Assistant Editor, *Our Past, Our Future – 100 Years of CPAs in Maryland: Maryland Association of Certified Public Accountants, Inc., 1901–2001*, Lutherville, MD, Maryland Association of Certified Public Accountants, Inc., pp. 161–163.

Loft, A. 1986. "Toward a Critical Understanding of Accounting: The Case of Cost Accounting in the U.K., 1914–1925," *Accounting, Organizations and Society*, 11: 137–169.

McMillan, K.P. May 1998a. "Efficient Accounting Systems: Justifying US Accounting Practice in an Unregulated Commercial Environment," *Accounting History*, NS 3: 115–142.

McMillan, K.P. May 1998b. "The Emergence of the U.S. Accounting Profession 1880–1900: A New Institutionism Perspective," Ph.D. Dissertation, London School of Economics and Political Science, The University of London.

McMillan, K.P. December 1998c. "The Science of Accounts: Bookkeeping Rooted in the Ideal of Science," *The Accounting Historians Journal*, 25: 1–33.

McMillan, K.P. March 1999. "The Institute of Accounts: A Community of the Competent," *Accounting, Business & Financial History*, 9: 7–28.

Makielski, Jr., S.J. 1973. *Beleaguered Minorities: Cultural Politics in America*, San Francisco: W.H. Freeman and Company.

Mandelbaum, S.J. 1965. *Boss Tweed's New York*, New York: John Wiley & Sons, Inc.

Mann, H.S. 1931. *Charles Ezra Sprague*, New York: New York University. Reprinted by Arno Press, New York, 1978.

"Massachusetts Institute of Accounts," June 1897. *Accountics: A Monthly Magazine for Office Men*, 1: 67. Reprinted in *Accountics, April 1897 to August 1900*, Part I: Volumes I and II, April 1897 to March 1898, Garland Publishing, Inc., New York, 1992.

"Mathematical Elucidation of Accounts.," June 1887. *The Office: A Practical Journal for Business Managers, Accountants and Office Men.*, 2: 103.

"The May Meeting.," June 1886. *The Office: A Practical Journal for Business Managers, Accountants and Office Men*, 1: 12.

"The Members of the Faculty of New York University School of Commerce, Accounts, and Finance," September 1900. *Business: The Office Paper and the Public Accountant*, 20: 412–413.

"'Men Loved Darkness Rather Than Light, For Their Deeds Were Evil.,'" January 12, 1901. *Commerce, Accounts & Finance*, 1: 1. Reprinted in *Commerce, Accounts & Finance*, Volume I–III, January–December 1901, New York: Garland Publishing, Inc., 1993.

Miller, P. and O'Leary, T. 1987. "Accounting and the Construction of the Governable Person," *Accounting, Organizations and Society*, 12: 235–265.

Miranti, P.J. August 1986a. "Robert H. Montgomery – A Leader of the Profession," *The CPA Journal*, 56: 106–108.

Miranti, Jr., P.J. Autumn 1986b. "Associationalism, Statism and Professional Regulation: Public Accountants and the Reform of the Financial Markets, 1896–1940," *Business History Review*, 60: 438–468.

Miranti, P.J. June 1988. "Professionalism and Nativism: The Competition in Securing Public Accounting Legislation in New York During the 1890s," *Social Science Quarterly*, 69: 361–380.

Miranti, Jr., P.J. Autumn 1989. "The Mind's Eye of Reform: The ICC's Bureau of Statistics and Accounts and a Vision of Regulation, 1887–1906," *Business History Review*, 63: 469–509.

Miranti, Jr., P.J. 1990. *Accountancy Comes of Age: The Development of an American Profession, 1886–1940*, Chapel Hill: The University of North Carolina Press.

Miranti, Jr., P.J. 1993a. "Introduction," in *Commerce, Accounts, & Finance*, Volumes I–III, January–December 1901, New York: Garland Publishing, Inc., pp. vii–xii.

Miranti, Jr., P.J. 1993b. "Patterns of Analysis in Accounting History," *Business and Economic History*, 22: 114–126.

Miranti, P.J. April 1996. "Birth of a Profession," *The CPA Journal*, 66: 14–18, 20, 72.

Miranti, Jr., P.J. and Goodman, L. 1996. "American Institute of Certified Public Accountants," in M. Chatfield and R. Vangermeersch, eds, *The History of Accounting: An International Encyclopedia*, New York: Garland Publishing, Inc., pp. 34–43.

Mirowski, P. 1989. *More Heat Than Light: Economics as Social Physics: Physics as Nature's Economics*, Cambridge: Cambridge University Press.

Mirowski, P., ed. 1994. *Natural Images in Economic Thought: "Markets Read in Tooth and Claw,"* Cambridge: Cambridge University Press.

"Mutual Associations for Book-keepers.," January 18, 1881. *The Book-Keeper.,* 2: 17–19. Reprinted in *The Book-Keeper and American Counting-Room,* Volume 1, July, 1880–December, 1881, Garland Publishing, Inc., New York, 1989.

"A National Institute of Accountants.," July 1883 *American Counting-room.,* 7: 37–38. Reprinted in *The Book-Keeper and American Counting-Room,* Volume 3, July, 1883–December, 1883, Garland Publishing, Inc., New York, 1989.

"National Society of Certified Public Accountants," August 1897. *Accountics: A Monthly Magazine for Office Men,* 1: 110. Reprinted in *Accountics, April 1897 to August 1900,* Part I: Volumes I and II, April 1897 to March 1898, Garland Publishing, Inc., New York, 1992.

"The National Society of Certified Public Accountants in the United States," January 1899. *The Public Accountant,* 1: 39.

"Nationalization of the Institute of Accounts," April 1897. *Accountics: A Monthly Magazine for Office Men,* 1: 14. Reprinted in *Accountics, April 1897 to August 1900,* Part I: Volumes I and II, April 1897 to March 1898, Garland Publishing, Inc., New York, 1992.

"New York Accountants' Headquarters," July 1897. *Accountics: A Monthly Magazine for Office Men,* 1: 82. Reprinted in *Accountics, April 1897 to August 1900,* Part I: Volumes I and II, April 1897 to March 1898, Garland Publishing, Inc., New York, 1992.

"New York Chapter," April 1897. *Accountics: A Monthly Magazine for Office Men,* 1: 14. Reprinted in *Accountics, April 1897 to August 1900,* Part I: Volumes I and II, April 1897 to March 1898, Garland Publishing, Inc., New York, 1992.

"New York Chapter," May 1898. *Accountics: The Office Magazine,* 3: 45. Reprinted in *Accountics, April 1897 to August 1900,* Part II: Volumes III, IV and V, April 1898 to December 1899, Garland Publishing, Inc., New York, 1992.

"New York Chapter of the Institute of Accounts," June 1899. *Accountics: The Office Magazine,* 4: 138. Reprinted in *Accountics, April 1897 to August 1900,* Part II: Volumes III, IV and V, April 1898 to December 1899, Garland Publishing, Inc., New York, 1992.

"New York Chapter of the Institute of Accounts," February 1900.

Accountics: The Office Magazine, 6: 25. Reprinted in *Accountics, April 1897 to August 1900*, Part III: Volumes VI and VII, January 1900 to August 1900, Garland Publishing, Inc., New York, 1992.

"New York State Society of Certified Public Accountants," April 1897. *Accountics: A Monthly Magazine for Office Men*, 1: 14–15. Reprinted in *Accountics, April 1897 to August 1900*, Part I: Volumes I and II, April 1897 to March 1898, Garland Publishing, Inc., New York, 1992.

New York State Society of Certified Public Accountants (NYSSCPA), September 1927. *New York State Society of Certified Public Accountants: 1927 Year Book*, New York: The New York State Society of Certified Public Accountants.

"New York University School of Commerce, Accounts & Finance," January 5, 1901a. *Commerce, Accounts & Finance*, 1: 16. Reprinted in *Commerce, Accounts & Finance*, Volume I–III, January–December 1901, New York: Garland Publishing, Inc., 1993.

"New York University School of Commerce, Accounts and Finance," February 2, 1901b. *Commerce, Accounts and Finance*, 1: 1. Reprinted in *Commerce, Accounts & Finance*, Volume I–III, January–December 1901, New York: Garland Publishing, Inc., 1993.

"Notes and Comments.," October 1883. *American Counting-room.*, 7: 234–237. Reprinted in *The Book-Keeper and American Counting-Room*, Volume 3, July, 1883–December, 1883, Garland Publishing, Inc., New York, 1989.

"Notes from the Editors' Table.," March 27, 1883. *The Book-Keeper.*, 6: 108–109. Reprinted in *The Book-Keeper and American Counting-Room*, Volume 2, January, 1882–June, 1883, Garland Publishing, Inc., New York, 1989.

Oakes, L.S. and Miranti, Jr., P.J. 1996. "Louis D. Brandeis and Standard Cost Accounting: A Study of the Construction of Historical Agency," *Accounting, Organizations and Society*, 21: 569–586.

"Official Journal," April 1897. *Accountics: A Monthly Magazine for Office Men*, 1: 16. Reprinted in *Accountics, April 1897 to August 1900*, Part I: Volumes I and II, April 1897 to March 1898, Garland Publishing, Inc., New York, 1992.

"Official Roster of Accountants' Associations," October 1897a. *Accountics: A Monthly Magazine for Office Men*, 2: end matter. Reprinted in *Accountics, April 1897 to August 1900*, Part I: Volumes I and II, April 1897 to March 1898, Garland Publishing, Inc., New York, 1992.

"Official Roster of Accountants' Associations," November 1897b. *Accountics: A Monthly Magazine for Office Men*, 2: end matter. Reprinted in *Accountics, April 1897 to August 1900*, Part I: Volumes I and II, April 1897 to March 1898, Garland Publishing, Inc., New York, 1992.

"Older Accounting Societies," 1941. In "Reports of the Executive Committee: Midyear Report," *1940 Yearbook of the American Institute of Accountants*, American Institute of Accountants, p. 125.

"Packard, Silas Sadler," 1893. *The National Cyclopaedia of American Biography*, Volume III, New York: James T. White & Company, p. 72.

Packard, S.S. February 1884. "As to the Method of Stating Things.," *American Counting-room.*, 8: 78–80. Reprinted in *The Book-Keeper and American Counting-Room*, Volume 4, January, 1884–December, 1884, Garland Publishing, Inc., New York, 1989.

Parsons, T. 1960. *Structure and Process in Modern Societies*, New York: The Free Press.

Paton, T.B. 1902, 1903. "The Negotiable Instruments Law," *Commerce, Accounts & Finance*, (January 1902) 4: 14–17, (February 1902) 4: 20–22, (March 1902) 4: 19–21, (April 1902) 4: 15–17, (May 1902) 4: 19–21, (June 1902) 4: 20–23, (July 1902) 4: 18–21, (September 1902) 4: 12–15, (April 1903) 5: 24–27), (October 1902) 4: 19–22, (November 1902) 4: 21–23; (January 1903) 5: 18–20, (March 1903) 5: 20–21, (May 1903) 5: 21–23. Reprinted in *Commerce, Accounts & Finance*, Volume IV–V, January, 1902–May, 1903, New York: Garland Publishing, Inc., 1993.

Paton, W.A. 1962. *Accounting Theory: With Special Reference to the Corporate Enterprise*, Houston, TX: Scholars Book Co. Reprinted 1973.

Paton, W.A. and Littleton, A.C. 1940. *An Introduction to Corporate Accounting Standards*, Monograph No. 3, American Accounting Association.

Perlmutter, P. 1996. *The Dynamics of American Ethnic, Religious, and Racial Group Life: An Interdisciplinary Overview*, Westport, CT: Praeger.

"A Philadelphia Chapter," April 1897. *Accountics: A Monthly Magazine for Office Men*, 1: 15. Reprinted in *Accountics, April 1897 to August 1900*, Part I: Volumes I and II, April 1897 to March 1898, Garland Publishing, Inc., New York, 1992.

Pierson, F.C. and Others. 1959. *The Education of American Business-men: A Study of University-College Programs in Business Adminis-tration*, New York, McGraw-Hill Book Company, Inc.

"Our Portraits.," February 27, 1883. *The Book-Keeper.*, 6: 65–67. Reprinted in *The Book-Keeper and American Counting-Room*, Volume 2, January, 1882–June, 1883, Garland Publishing, Inc., New York, 1989.

Previts, G.J. and Merino, B.D. 1979. *A History of Accounting in America: An Historical Interpretation of the Cultural Significance of Accounting*, New York: A Ronald Press Publication, John Wiley & Sons.

"Progressive Accounting," March 1895. *Business: The Office Paper*, 15: 84.

Raymond, F. July 1883. "Checking Embezzlement in Tax Collec-tions.," *American Counting-room.*, 7: 18–19. Reprinted in *The Book-Keeper and American Counting-Room*, Volume 3, July, 1883–December, 1883, Garland Publishing, Inc., New York, 1989.

"Real Estate Accounts.," March 1884. *American Counting-room.*, 8: 165–166. Reprinted in *The Book-Keeper and American Counting-Room*, Volume 4, January, 1884–December, 1884, Garland Pub-lishing, Inc., New York, 1989.

Reckitt, E. May 1940. "History of Accountancy in the State of Illinois," *The Journal of Accountancy*, 69: 376–380.

Reckitt, E. 1953. *Reminiscences of Early Days of the Accounting Pro-fession in Illinois*, Chicago: Illinois Society of Certified Public Accountants.

"Reports of the Executive Committee: Midyear Report," 1941. *1940 Yearbook of the American Institute of Accountants*, American Insti-tute of Accountants, pp. 120–129.

Richardson, A.J. June 1989. "Canada's Accounting Elite: 1880–1930," *The Accounting Historians Journal*, 16: 1–21.

Robert, R. November 1955. "The Accountant in Literature," *Accoun-tancy*, 66 (17 New Series): 416–418.

Robert, R. March 1957. "The Accountant in Literature," *The Journal of Accountancy*, 103: 64–66.

Roberts, A.R. May 1987. "The 'Other' Public Accounting Organi-zations," *Journal of Accountancy*, 163: 41–42.

Romeo, G.C. and Kyj, L.S. June 1998. "The Forgotten Accounting Association: The Institute of Accounts," *The Accounting Historians Journal*, 25: 29–55.

Romeo, G.C. and Kyj, L.S. December 2000. "Anson O. Kittredge: Early Accounting Pioneer," *The Accounting Historians Journal*, 27: 117–143.

Rosenberg, C.E. 1987. *The Care of Strangers: The Rise of America's Hospital System*, New York: Basic Books, Inc., Publishers.

Ross, D. 1991. *The Origins of American Social Science*, Cambridge: Cambridge University Press.

Roy, R.H. and MacNeill, J.H. September 1966. "Horizons for a Profession: The Common Body of Knowledge for CPAs," *The Journal of Accountancy*, 122: 38–50.

Safely, J. June 7, 1881. "Clerks' and Accountants' Co-operative Credit Society.," *The Book-Keeper.*, 2: 120–121. Reprinted in *The Book-Keeper and American Counting-Room*, Volume 1, July, 1880–December, 1881, Garland Publishing, Inc., New York, 1989.

Sass, S.A. 1982. *The Pragmatic Imagination: A History of the Wharton School, 1881–1981*, Philadelphia: University of Pennsylvania Press.

Scott, D.M. 1983. "The Profession That Vanished: Public Lecturing in Mid-Nineteenth-Century America," in Gerald L. Geison, ed., *Professions and Professional Ideologies in America*, Chapel Hill: The University of North Carolina Press, pp. 12–28.

"Selden R. Hopkins . . .," November 23, 1880. *The Book-Keeper.*, 1: 159. Reprinted in *The Book-Keeper and American Counting-Room*, Volume 1, July, 1880–December, 1881, Garland Publishing, Inc., New York, 1989.

Shackleton, K. 1995. "Scottish Chartered Accountants: Internal and External Political Relationships, 1853–1916," *Accounting, Auditing & Accountability Journal*, 8: 18–46.

"Silas Sadler Packard," October 1898. *Accountics: The Office Magazine*, 3: 135. Reprinted in *Accountics, April 1897 to August 1900*, Part II: Volumes III, IV and V, April 1898 to December 1899, Garland Publishing, Inc., New York, 1992.

Skowronek, S. 1982. *Building a New American State: The Expansion of National Administrative Capacities, 1877–1920*, Cambridge: Cambridge University Press.

Slocombe, J. 1882, 1883. "Auditing.," *The Book-Keeper*. (December 19) 5: 398–401; (January 2) 6: 5–7, (January 16) 6: 20–23. Reprinted in *The Book-Keeper and American Counting-Room*, Volume 2, January, 1882–June, 1883, Garland Publishing, Inc., New York, 1989.

Smykay, E.W. 1955. "The National Association of Railroad and Utility

Commissioners as the Originators and Promoters of Public Policy for Public Utilities," Ph.D. Dissertation. University of Wisconsin.

Society Release. May 1959. "Dedication of Haskins' Memorial Room," *The New York Certified Public Accountant*, 29: 357–360.

Spence, C.C. 1970. *Mining Engineers & the American West: The Lace-Boot Brigade, 1849–1933*, New Haven: Yale University Press.

Sprague, C.E. 1880a. "The Algebra of Accounts.," *The Book-Keeper.* (July 20) 1: 2–4, 1: 19–22 (August 3), 1: 34–35, 44–48 (August 17), 1: 51–53 (August 31). Reprinted in *The Book-Keeper and American Counting-Room*, Volume 1, July, 1880–December, 1881, Garland Publishing, Inc., New York, 1989.

Sprague, C.E. October 12, 1880b. "The Detection of Errors in Balance-Sheets.," *The Book-Keeper.*, 1: 97–101. Reprinted in *The Book-Keeper and American Counting-Room*, Volume 1, July, 1880–December, 1881, Garland Publishing, Inc., New York, 1989.

Sprague, C.E. September 1883. "Embezzlements and Accountability.," *American Counting-room.*, 7: 149–154. Reprinted in *The Book-Keeper and American Counting-Room*, Volume 3, July, 1883–December, 1883, Garland Publishing, Inc., New York, 1989.

Sprague, C.E. November 1889. "Outlay and Income.," *The Office: A Practical Journal of Business Management, Office Routine and the Art of Advertising*, 7: 207–208.

Sprague, C.E. January 1898a. "Logismography I," *Accountics: A Monthly Magazine for Office Men*, 2: 73–75. Reprinted in *Accountics, April 1897 to August 1900*, Part I: Volumes I and II, April 1897 to March 1898, Garland Publishing, Inc., New York, 1992.

Sprague, C.E. February 1898b. "Logismography II," *Accountics: The Office Magazine*, 2: 117–121. Reprinted in *Accountics, April 1897 to August 1900*, Part I: Volumes I and II, April 1897 to March 1898, Garland Publishing, Inc., New York, 1992.

Sprague, C.E. February 2, 1901. "The General Principles of the Science of Accounts," *Commerce, Accounts & Finance*, 1: 3–5. Reprinted in *Commerce, Accounts & Finance*, Volume I–III, January–December 1901, New York: Garland Publishing, Inc., 1993.

Sprague, C.E. 1907. *The Philosophy of Accounts*. Reprinted by Scholars Book Co., Houston, 1972. [Author's note: Almost all of Sprague (1907) likely first published in parts of 1907 and 1908 in a serialized format in *The Journal of Accountancy* (see, e.g., the reference to Charles Sprague and that journal in *Accountants' Index*, 1921, p. 1377).]

Stacey, N.A.H. January 1958. "The Accountant in Literature," *The Accounting Review*, 33: 102–105.

Starr, P. 1982. *The Social Transformation of American Medicine*, New York: Basic Books, Inc., Publishers.

Stevens, R. 1971. *American Medicine and the Public Interest*, New Haven: Yale University Press.

Taylor, N. [pseud.]. June 19, 1883a. "De Institute an Formed.," *The Book-Keeper.*, 6: 196–197. Reprinted in *The Book-Keeper and American Counting-Room*, Volume 2, January, 1882–June, 1883, Garland Publishing, Inc., New York, 1989.

Taylor, N. [pseud.]. July 1883b. "I.A. & B.C.M.U.S.N.A.", *American Counting-room.*, 7: 36–37. Reprinted in *The Book-Keeper and American Counting-Room*, Volume 3, July, 1883–December, 1883, Garland Publishing, Inc., New York, 1989.

Taylor, N. [pseud.] March 1884. "I.A. & B.C.M.U.S.N.A.", *American Counting-room.* 8: 170–171. Reprinted in *The Book-Keeper and American Counting-Room*, Volume 4, January, 1884–December, 1884, Garland Publishing, Inc., New York, 1989.

"Technical Discussions.," 1882. *The Book-Keeper.* (July 4) 5: 209–214, (September 12) 5: 291–294. Reprinted in *The Book-Keeper and American Counting-Room*, Volume 2, January, 1882–June, 1883, Garland Publishing, Inc., New York, 1989.

"Third Annual Convention of the Institute of Accounts," June 1899. *Accountics: The Office Magazine*, 4: 138–139. Reprinted in *Accountics, April 1897 to August 1900*, Part II: Volumes III, IV and V, April 1898 to December 1899, Garland Publishing, Inc., New York, 1992.

Thompson, J.E. 1996. "Paton, William Andrew (1889–1991)," in M. Chatfield and R. Vangermeersch, eds, *The History of Accounting: An International Encyclopedia*, New York: Garland Publishing, Inc., pp. 453–454.

Tinker, A. Spring 1984. "Theories of the State and the State of Accounting: Economic Reductionism and Political Voluntarism in Accounting Regulation Theory," *Journal of Accounting and Public Policy*, 3: 55–74.

Tucker, III, J.J. and Lordi, F.C. June 1997. "Early Efforts of the U.S. Public Accounting Profession to Investigate the Use of Statistical Sampling," *The Accounting Historians Journal*, 24: 93–116.

U.S. Bureau of the Census. 1975. *Historical Statistics of the United States: Colonial Times to 1970: Part I*, Bicentennial Edition, Washington, D.C.: U.S. Department of Commerce.

U.S. Census Office. 1902. *Census Reports, Volume II: Twelfth Census of the United States, Taken in the Year 1900, Population, Part II*, W.R. Merriam, Director; W.C. Hunt, Chief Statistician for Population, Washington, D.C.: Department of the Interior.

Walker, S.P. 1988. *The Society of Accountants in Edinburgh 1854–1914: A Study of Recruitment to a New Profession*, New York: Garland Publishing Inc.

"Washington Chapter of the Institute of Accounts," January 1898. *Accountics: A Monthly Magazine for Office Men*, 2: 93. Reprinted in *Accountics, April 1897 to August 1900*, Part I: Volumes I and II, April 1897 to March 1898, Garland Publishing, Inc., New York, 1992.

Webster, N.E., Compiler. 1954. *The American Association of Public Accountants: Its First Twenty Years, 1886–1906*, New York: American Institute of Accountants.

Wescott, S.H. and Seiler, R.E. 1986. *Women in the Accounting Profession*, New York: Markus Wiener Publishing, Inc.

Whitely, R. 1986. "The Transformation of Business Finance into Financial Economics: The Role of Academic Expansion and Changes in U.S. Capital Markets," *Accounting, Organizations and Society*, 11: 171–192.

Wiebe, R.H. 1967. *The Search for Order, 1877–1920*, New York: Hill and Wang [Farrar, Straus and Giroux, LLC].

Wiebe, R.H. 1975. *The Segmented Society: An Introduction to the Meaning of America*, New York: Oxford University Press.

Wilensky, H.L. September 1964. "The Professionalization of Everyone?," *The American Journal of Sociology*, 70: 137–158.

Wilkins, M. 1989. *The History of Foreign Investment in the United States*, Cambridge, MA: Harvard University Press.

Wilkinson, G. 1903. "The C.P.A. Movement," *The Business World: An Office Magazine*, (September) 23: 414–416, (October) 23: 460–463.

Wilkinson, G. May 1908. "The Advantages of Organization to the Accountant," *The Journal of Accountancy*, 6: 45–56.

Wilkinson, G. September 1928. "The Genesis of the C.P.A. Movement," *The Certified Public Accountant*, 8: 261–266, 279–281, 284–285.

"William Bainbridge Jaudon," May 1897 *Accountics: A Monthly Magazine for Office Men*, 1: 47. Reprinted in *Accountics, April 1897 to August 1900*, Part I: Volumes I and II, April 1897 to March 1898, Garland Publishing, Inc., New York, 1992.

Willmott, H. 1986. "Organising the Profession: A Theoretical and Historical Examination of the Development of the Major Accountancy Bodies in the U.K.," *Accounting, Organizations and Society*, 11: 555–580.

Zeff, S.A. July 1984. "Some Junctures in the Evolution of the Process of Establishing Accounting Principles in the U.S.A.: 1917–1972," *The Accounting Review*, 59: 447–468.

Index

Page numbers in italics refer to or include a relevant figure.